Praise for *20/20 Foresight*

"The decision-making processes described in *20/20 Foresight* will be very valuable to anyone trying to develop a cogent strategy and business plan for a new venture. Hugh Courtney's work has given us a great start with a sophisticated method for managing a multivariate opportunity."

> —Kenneth J. Conway, President, Millennium Predictive Medicine

"*20/20 Foresight* is an excellent book that unravels the mysteries of business uncertainty and its effects on strategic decision making. Hugh Courtney highlights strategic trade-offs and presents best-in-class toolkits. A great guide for CEOs and strategists."

> —Edward Roberts, Founder and Chairman, MIT Entrepreneurship
> Center, and Cofounder of KnowledgeCube Ventures

"*20/20 Foresight* is the closest thing that I have seen to a corporate crystal ball. Hugh Courtney provides valuable lessons and practical tools for deciphering the future and creating winning business strategies."

> —James M. Klingensmith, Group Executive Vice President,
> Highmark, Inc.

"Instead of taking the traditional 'all-or-nothing' view of uncertainty, this book explains how to think about the different levels of uncertainty—and why they have distinct, powerful implications for strategy making. You had better read this book if you think your company has room to improve in this area."

> —Pankaj Ghemawat, Jaime and Josefina Chua Tiampo Professor
> of Business Administration, Harvard Business School

20|20
FORESIGHT

To Pam and Joseph

20|20 FORESIGHT

Crafting Strategy in an Uncertain World

HUGH COURTNEY

HARVARD BUSINESS SCHOOL PRESS
BOSTON, MASSACHUSETTS

Requests for permission to use or reproduce material from this book should be directed to permissions@hbsp.harvard.edu, or mailed to Permissions, Harvard Business School Publishing, 60 Harvard Way, Boston, Massachusetts 02163.

Library of Congress Cataloging-in-Publication Data

Courtney, Hugh, 1963–
    20/20 foresight : crafting strategy in an uncertain world / Hugh Courtney.
      p. cm.
    Includes bibliographical references and index.
    ISBN 1-57851-266-2 (alk. paper)
    1. Strategic planning. I. Title: Twenty/twenty foresight. II. Title.

  HD30.28 .C6965 2001
  658.4'012—dc21   2001024174

The paper used in this publication meets the requirements of the American National Standard for Permanence of Paper for Publications and Documents in Libraries and Archives Z39.48-1992.

Contents

Preface

IN THE FALL OF 1994, a group of McKinsey partners met in Paris to discuss the state of the firm's business strategy consulting practice. The group reached a troubling consensus: The strategy development approaches taught by most business schools and used by most major corporations were outdated and inappropriate for most business strategy issues.

The group discussed dozens of recent case examples, trying to determine why these traditional strategy approaches so often failed. Time and again, high uncertainty appeared to be the root cause.

The strategic-planning and decision-making approaches used by most companies assumed that, with the right analysis, the future could be forecast with enough precision to identify the right strategy. Yet rapid change and high levels of uncertainty were making it increasingly difficult for companies to develop such forecasts. As a result, many companies were abandoning analytical rigor altogether when making strategy decisions, while others were burying uncertainty in meaningless point forecasts. In both cases, strategies emerged that neither addressed the threats nor captured the opportunities that high uncertainty brings. There had to be a better approach.

As the Paris meeting adjourned, the group agreed to launch McKinsey's Strategy Theory Initiative (STI), a multiyear research effort designed to identify, develop, and disseminate such an approach. The STI was made up of several project teams, each focusing on a particular aspect of strategy theory and practice, and eventually involving more than sixty McKinsey consultants, several academics, and over 100 companies on six continents. One team was devoted to the study of strategy under high uncertainty. This was the team for me, as I was eager to help my own clients and consulting teams overcome the difficulties they faced when making decisions under uncertainty.

As a former academic economist, I knew that business practitioners had only begun to tap into the vast—but virtually impenetrable—academic literature on strategy under uncertainty. My initial efforts, then, focused on translating insights from this work into practical strategy tools. Yet this effort was largely disappointing. Academic books and articles had very useful things to say about particular tools, such as real options valuation and scenario planning, but none of these tools seemed universally applicable across the wide range of strategy problems facing my clients. There was no easy one-size-fits-all solution that could be translated from theory into practice. Business strategists needed new theory *and* new practices if they wanted to make better strategy choices.

The team supplemented its findings from the academic literature with new case studies of companies that had thrived and failed in uncertain environments, and field-tested new ideas, tools, and frameworks with dozens of our clients. In the end, our academic advisors, McKinsey colleagues, and especially our clients taught us quite a bit about how to craft winning strategies in an uncertain world. The result was a new, integrated theory and approach to strategy under uncertainty, from option generation to analysis, decision making, and ongoing strategic management.

This book describes our approach. It is already helping our consulting teams and clients make systematically better strategy choices when faced with high uncertainty. I hope, and believe, that your company can make better choices, too, if it follows our approach. That is why I wrote this book.

ACKNOWLEDGMENTS

This book would not exist were it not for McKinsey's unfailing commitment to the STI, and the STI would not exist were it not for the outstanding leadership provided by a small band of committed partners. Kevin Coyne and Somu Subramaniam led the entire STI effort, and they helped develop many of its initial results on strategy under uncertainty. In addition, Jane Kirkland and Patrick Viguerie led the strategy-under-uncertainty project team, and they codeveloped many of the ideas and examples presented in this book.

While I alone worked to translate the STI results into this book, and thus I am solely responsible for its content (including any errors or omissions), I consider Kevin, Somu, Jane, and Patrick to be my four co-authors. I thank them for their enormous contributions to my understanding of strategy under uncertainty, and for being model colleagues.

Other members of the STI research team made significant contributions to our work on uncertainty. Bill Barnett, Eric Beinhocker, David Benello, Trish Clifford, Renée Dye, John Hagel, Dag Sundström, and Lo-Ping Yeh, in particular, deserve special mention. This group served as an ongoing sounding board for new ideas and frameworks.

Several other McKinsey colleagues allowed me to borrow liberally from their ideas and research efforts when developing sections of this book. I have cited their contributions at relevant points within the text, but they should also be acknowledged here. I thank Petri Allas, Tom Copeland, Phil Keenan, Keith Leslie, David McDonald, Ramesh Venkataraman, and especially Max Michaels for their work on real options; John Hagel, Joe Heel, Marc Singer, Somu Subramaniam, and Lo-Ping Yeh for their work on the shape-versus-adapt choice; Johan Ahlberg, Henrik Arwidi, Bill Barnett, Shona Brown, Michael Dickstein, Chandru Krishnamurthy, Alex Rogers, and Patrick Viguerie for their work on strategic planning and decision making under high uncertainty; Eric Beinhocker for his work on complex adaptive systems; Andrew Doman, Maurice Glucksman, Jin-Goon Kim, Paul Langley, Hendrik Sabert, Olivier Sibony, Jayant Sinha, Paolo Timoni, and Nhuoc-Lan Tu for their work on system dynamics and management flight simulators; Bill Barnett for his work on contingent road maps; and Bill Barnett and Patrick Viguerie for their work on game theory.

Several academics also helped shape the book's ideas as they were being formed in early drafts, including Ralph Biggadike, Jonathan Doh, Kathleen Eisenhardt, Pankaj Ghemawat, Ehud Houminer, Barry Nalebuff, Rhonda Reger, and Paul Schoemaker.

While these academic and McKinsey colleagues all played vital roles in shaping the book's content, my clients (and my colleagues' clients) played the most important roles. While client confidentiality arrangements prevent me from naming names, you know who you are. Thank you for your endless supply of practical ideas, willingness to experiment with new approaches, and courage to act upon new ideas. I hope you have enjoyed and valued our work together as much as I have.

As the STI uncertainty work evolved from the concept development to the book-writing stage, other people made substantial contributions. McKinsey's Strategy Practice funded my book-writing efforts, allowing me to devote substantial blocks of uninterrupted time to getting the job done. I thank the Strategy Practice's leaders, Bill Huyett and Charles Roxburgh, for their belief in this project and their willingness to "bet" on its outcome. In addition, Sallie Honeychurch, Denis Konouck, and Sandra Lummus provided superb research and administrative support as cases were developed, facts were checked, and references were identified. My assistant, Tonya Flores, also provided outstanding administrative support throughout the entire book-writing phase, and she helped keep my spirits up on the inevitable dark days.

In addition to those listed above, several others provided detailed comments on early book drafts that helped me refine ideas and clarify their exposition. Michael Chapman, Michael Cragg, Renate Imoberdorf-Lingnau, and Dan Lovallo all provided useful comments. I also owe special thanks to the five anonymous readers who reviewed an earlier draft of this book for the Harvard Business School Press. Their thoughtful comments led me to significantly restructure the book's material. I believe, and I hope they will agree, that this new structure substantially clarifies the book's primary messages.

It has also been my great pleasure to work with Erik Calonius. Erik has read and reread the entire manuscript numerous times, each time coming back with thoughtful, clarifying edits. As I worked through Erik's edits, I found myself constantly thinking, "Now why didn't I write it that way in the first place?" When people ask me what I learned from the book-writing process, I always say, "Erik taught me how to write." Thanks for this invaluable lesson, Erik, and thank you, too, for being such a gifted motivator.

Others also provided valuable editorial support. Saul Rosenberg and Joan Magretta helped Jane Kirkland, Patrick Viguerie, and me shape some of the unformed work from our preliminary STI research into a lead article for the *Harvard Business Review*. The positive response to this article, along with encouragement from Saul and Joan, led us to first consider publishing a book on this topic.

I also owe special thanks to the entire Harvard Business School Press team for its support of this project. It has added significant value throughout the entire book-writing process, from my initial proposal to the first draft, and from peer review to final manuscript production. In particular, I thank Marjorie Williams for her belief in this project from the very start, and Nikki Sabin and Melinda Merino for seeing it through to a successful finish. Sylvia Weedman was another essential member of the editorial team, and Jill Connor led the editorial-production team. Thank you, Marjorie, Nikki, Melinda, Sylvia, and Jill for your professionalism, patience, and good humor.

Finally, I thank my wife, Pamela Loprest, and son, Joseph, for everything, because without their love and support there would be no book. Pam and Joseph, this book is dedicated to you.

1

CRAFTING STRATEGY IN AN UNCERTAIN WORLD

THE BUSINESS WORLD is changing fast. Remember when the "future" was a year away, or three years—or even five years? No longer. Lewis E. Platt, former Hewlett-Packard chief executive officer (CEO), argues, "Anyone who tells you they have a 5- or 10-year plan is probably crazy."[1] Old economy or new, you'd be hard-pressed to find any business leaders who disagree.

With rapid change comes uncertainty. And with uncertainty comes risk—and great opportunities. If you bet big today, for instance, you may fundamentally reshape an emerging market to your advantage. Or you may suffer losses that throw your company into bankruptcy. If you wait for the uncertainty surrounding a possible opportunity to disappear, on the other hand, you may avoid making some foolhardy mistakes—or you may lose your first-mover advantages to a more aggressive competitor.

In choosing strategies under uncertainty, there are no easy answers. Yet many business strategists make it harder than it has to be, simply by relying on outdated strategic-planning and decision-making approaches. These "tried-and-true" approaches, designed to optimize strategic decision making in predictable environments, systematically fail in times of high uncertainty, as we are experiencing today.

1

Take the typical strategic-planning and decision-making process, which is still extensively used by most large corporations, consulting firms, and M.B.A. programs. This process is built around the *business case.* Managers describe a potential investment or other strategic action in great detail, and then they build a "fact-based" case to estimate its expected economic return. Since the return to any strategy depends on its impact on future cash flows, the process is naturally forward-looking— and thus reliant on sound forecasts of such variables as market size and share, prices, and productivity.

Foresight—an accurate view of the future—is essential in generating the best forecasts and making the right strategy choices. The typical process assumes that the strategists possess the foresight to translate their knowledge of the future into *point forecasts* of key value drivers. These point forecasts allow for precise estimates of net present value (NPV) and other financial measures, which, in turn, determine which strategy will deliver the highest return.[2]

In addition, the typical process assumes that a deep, analytical under-standing of today's market environment and today's company capabili-ties is the key to developing foresight about the future. For example, industry analysis frameworks, like Porter's Five Forces, are at the heart of most prototypical processes because it is implicitly assumed that understanding the microeconomic drivers of today's market environment is essential to understanding the strategies that will win in tomorrow's market.[3]

In relatively stable market environments—environments character-ized by limited uncertainty—these are reasonable assumptions. In such markets, for example, the best indicators of *next year's* customer needs, competitor conduct, and technology standards are *this year's* customer needs, competitor conduct, and technology standards. Likewise, in stable market environments, forecasts of future value drivers *can* be accurately extrapolated from current value drivers. In such cases, strategists with foresight should be able to generate accurate point forecasts.

But in times of great uncertainty, this process is marginally helpful at best, and at worst, downright dangerous: The traditional process encour-ages managers, who are trying to generate point-forecast assumptions, to ignore whatever uncertainties they may find. As a result, strategies emerge that neither manage the risks nor take advantage of the opportu-nities that present themselves in highly uncertain times.

20/20 FORESIGHT

It's time to get realistic about strategy under uncertainty. The truth is that foresight does not emerge solely from the painstaking analyses of *current* market environments. Nor does it emerge from studying the "perfect" forecasting tool, if it existed: a crystal ball that would make all your uncertainties disappear. Rather, the real issue is how to make the *best* strategy choices you can, accepting the ever presence of uncertainty.

For that reason, this book starts with a very simple but powerful idea: If you want to make better strategy choices under uncertainty, then you have to understand the uncertainty you are facing. Instead of burying uncertainties in meaningless base case forecasts—or avoiding rigorous analysis of uncertainties altogether—you must embrace uncertainty, explore it, slice it, dice it, get to know it. If you do this well, you will reach a wonderful goal: *20/20 foresight.*

Having 20/20 foresight doesn't mean that you can always make flawless future predictions. Even with 20/20 foresight you'll be occasionally blindsided, and you'll take some missteps along the way. But think of 20/20 foresight as you do 20/20 eyesight: People with 20/20 vision don't have perfect eyesight. They can't see the craters on the moon without a telescope, or a bird on the tallest tree without a pair of binoculars. But they can see the best that human beings can, given our natural physiological constraints.

Likewise, 20/20 foresight isn't perfect forward vision, but it is surprisingly clear, given the number of uncertainties that are beyond any human's ability to foresee. Business strategists with 20/20 foresight are not prescient, but they are doing the best they can to see the future.

THE FOUR LEVELS OF RESIDUAL UNCERTAINTY

To be sure, 20/20 foresight has always been the goal of the best strategic-planning and decision-making processes. Then why have strategists so often fallen short of the goal? You could blame poor execution—inadequate data collection and analysis, inappropriate forecasting techniques, misinterpretations of emerging trends, and so forth. But that's only part of the problem. The biggest problem is that most managers simply don't understand what it means to have 20/20 foresight under uncertainty.

Rather than seeing uncertainty as something that can be analyzed, most managers accept a *binary* view of uncertainty.[4] That is, they believe that uncertainty is nonexistent in some situations, in which case point forecasts can be made with ease. For all other situations, they believe uncertainty exists; and when it does, it is like a steel wall—completely impenetrable and opaque.

It is this binary view of uncertainty that leads many business strategists to either embrace point-forecast based methods entirely or, racked with frustration, decide to abandon systematic, analytical rigor altogether and go with their "intuition." Too bad, because in this fast-changing world, intuition based on previous experience may be dead-on wrong. In uncertain times, neither approach generates the foresight necessary to make sound strategic decisions.

The truth is that uncertainty is not an all-or-nothing phenomenon. Even in the most uncertain business environments, analysis can usually penetrate the uncertainty and withdraw strategically relevant information. It is this *residual uncertainty*—the uncertainty left after the best possible analysis to separate the unknown from the unknowable—that defines 20/20 foresight. If you can identify the residual uncertainty in your business environment, you can achieve 20/20 foresight.

For those in search of foresight, the good news is that residual uncertainty always takes one of four—and only four—forms. The lowest level of uncertainty, called Level 1, is so low that the traditional methods that employ point forecasts can be used with great success. On the other hand, the highest level, called Level 4, is a situation where analysis cannot even bound the range of possibilities, let alone generate reliable point forecasts of key value drivers.

Between these two extremes, however, are Levels 2 and 3, the levels of uncertainty most likely to face managers. In Level 3 situations, managers can bound the range of possible outcomes. And in Level 2 situations, managers can take this one step further and identify a set of distinct possible outcomes, one of which will occur.

To illustrate the four levels, consider the following example. Suppose you work for a telecommunications company and have been charged with introducing high-speed Internet access via digital subscriber lines (DSL) in a new market area. If you are asked what the DSL penetration rate will be in this market three years from now, there are only four possible forms your answer might take:

- "DSL will penetrate X% of the market in three years," if you face Level 1 uncertainty

- "DSL will penetrate either X%, Y%, or Z% of the market in three years," if you face Level 2 uncertainty

- "DSL will penetrate somewhere between X% and Z% of the market in three years," if you face Level 3 uncertainty

- "I don't know, and there's no reliable way to forecast what the range of possible DSL penetration rates will be in three years," if you face Level 4 uncertainty

This example is not unique. Take any strategic decision facing your company and ask how much can be known today about the future value drivers—like customer buying behavior, regulatory rulings, technology shifts, and competitor conduct—that will determine the success of your strategy. Your answers will always take one of the four generic forms outlined above. Decision makers always face one of the four levels of residual uncertainty.

The four levels of residual uncertainty constitute this book's core framework. The four levels framework defines the different degrees of foresight possible in an uncertain world. It will be fully developed in chapter 2.

But the four levels framework is more than just a foresight gauge. All aspects of strategy—including the processes you use to formulate strategy as well as the actual investments you make to implement your strategy—should be tailored to the level of residual uncertainty you face. Identifying your level of residual uncertainty, in fact, will help you determine the best possible answers to the five questions, seen below, that define strategy under uncertainty.

STRATEGY UNDER UNCERTAINTY:
FIVE KEY QUESTIONS

As my colleagues and I at McKinsey have worked with clients across numerous industries—old and new economy alike—we have identified a set of five common issues that make strategy making under high uncertainty differ from strategy making under low uncertainty. Each issue raises a fundamental question about strategy under uncertainty that we have addressed time and again in the past several years. Chapters 3 through 7 present what we have learned about the best possible answers to these questions. Table 1-1 summarizes the five questions and the chapter that addresses each one.

Shape or Adapt?

In a stable market environment with low uncertainty and a slow pace of change, companies typically try to find the best fit between existing market opportunities and company capabilities when formulating strategies. They take industry structure and competitive conduct as it is, and then they choose a strategy that *adapts* to the market environment. Much less attention is usually devoted to assessing strategies that might fundamentally *shape* industry structure and conduct to create changes that play to a company's advantages. This emphasis on adapting rather than shaping is natural in stable market environments, where key elements of industry structure and conduct—such as technology platforms, regulations, competitors, and customer purchasing patterns—appear to be locked-in and difficult to change.

In more uncertain markets, however, many of these key elements may be ill defined and in flux, and hence susceptible to being shaped. A company's decision to adopt a new technology, for instance, may help establish that technology as the industry standard.

Under what circumstances should companies attempt to proactively shape uncertain industry structure and conduct, and when is it better to reactively adapt to industry changes over time? Chapter 3 addresses this fundamental strategy-under-uncertainty question. Several factors come into play, and there is no one-size-fits-all answer for all companies in all situations. Perhaps the most important factor—and the one largely ignored—is the level of residual uncertainty facing the decision maker.

Now or Later?

Whether you choose to shape or adapt, strategy invariably involves making at least some major commitments that are hard to reverse. These include acquisitions, capital investments, and choices about the design of the business system. The timing of such commitments is often the key to building and sustaining competitive advantage.

Table 1-1 Strategy under Uncertainty: Five Key Questions

Issue	Question	Chapter
1. Strategists have traditionally crafted strategies that adapt to the market environment, but there are often greater opportunities to shape the environment under high uncertainty.	Under what circumstances should companies attempt to shape industry structure and conduct, and when is it better to reactively adapt to industry changes over time?	Chapter 3, "Shape or Adapt?"
2. When strategists postpone decisions when faced with high uncertainty, they may be able to access better information before making major commitments, but they also may open up opportunities for competitors to capture first-mover advantages.	Under what circumstances should companies postpone or stage major commitments over time, and when is it better to make more immediate, full-scale commitments?	Chapter 4, "Now or Later?"
3. Although focused strategies that bet on a particular uncertain outcome often offer the highest expected returns, they are usually riskier than more diversified strategies.	Under what circumstances should companies craft strategies that are robust across the range of possible future outcomes, and when should they prefer more focused strategies?	Chapter 5, "Focus or Diversify?"
4. The traditional strategy toolkit is of limited value when crafting strategies under high uncertainty.	Which specific tools and frameworks should business strategists use to supplement the traditional strategy toolkit?	Chapter 6, "New Tools and Frameworks?" Appendix: "The Uncertainty Toolkit"
5. The typical strategic-planning and decision-making process limits the ability of companies to change direction in response to—or in anticipation of—new opportunities or threats.	What alternative processes should companies use to monitor and update their strategies over time?	Chapter 7, "New Strategic-Planning and Decision-Making Processes?"

When faced with high uncertainty, deciding when to commit is no easy task. A company that postpones a commitment may learn more about the economic viability of its proposed strategy as market uncertainties unfold, and it may thus be able to make a wiser, less risky decision in the future. On the other hand, postponement may also increase the risk that a more aggressive competitor will preempt a company's proposed strategy.

Business strategists must manage this trade-off between gathering more information but potentially losing an opportunity when choosing when to commit under high uncertainty. In contrast, deciding when to commit under low uncertainty is relatively straightforward. Delays increase the probability of competitive preemption while providing limited incremental information about the future. The prescription: Commit now.

Under what circumstances should companies postpone or stage major commitments over time, and when is it better to make more immediate, full-scale commitments? Chapter 4 addresses this "now or later" question. Applying lessons and tools from recent work on *real options,* chapter 4 shows how understanding the levels of residual uncertainty and competitive intensity in a market environment is the key to the better timing of commitment decisions.

Focus or Diversify?

When faced with high uncertainty, a focused strategy might enable a company to reap the highest upside returns in some scenarios, but it may also expose it to large downside losses in other scenarios. Betting on one technology rather that another is one example. If a company wants to ensure against such downside losses, it might assemble a more diversified *strategy portfolio*—for example, making a series of smaller bets on each feasible technology. This insurance may decrease the company's exposure, but at the price of a lower expected return.

When determining how focused their strategies should be under high uncertainty, business strategists must manage this risk/return trade-off. In contrast, under low uncertainty, no such trade-off exists. If key value drivers can be forecast with great precision, diversifying one's strategy portfolio to limit downside risk makes no sense. In such circumstances, a company might still maintain a diversified set of businesses or products in a market. But the rationale for such diversification would most likely be revenue and cost synergies across business or product lines, not risk management.

Under what circumstances should companies craft strategies that are robust across the range of possible future outcomes, and when should they prefer more focused strategies? Chapter 5 addresses this "focus or diversify" question. A number of company-specific factors should drive this choice, including assets, capabilities, and attitudes toward risk. A capital-constrained start-up, for example, can rarely afford to hedge its bets across competing technologies. But a big company, like Cisco Systems, can. Just because a company can successfully hedge doesn't mean it should, however. External market conditions, especially the nature and level of residual uncertainty, are often the deciding factors.

New Tools and Frameworks?

Under low uncertainty, the traditional strategy toolkit described earlier—including frameworks like Porter's Five Forces and tools like discounted cash flow models—works well. This toolkit is designed to generate strategic insights in relatively stable market environments. But if your goal is 20/20 foresight under higher levels of uncertainty, it is not up to the task.

In recent years, a number of high-uncertainty tools and frameworks have been offered as solutions to this foresight problem. But to date, this new toolkit has produced inconsistent results at best. Why? Each element of the toolkit has been oversold, leading companies to apply the wrong tool to the wrong problem at the wrong time. How many times have we heard that real options or scenario planning or game theory or complex adaptive systems is *the* solution to generating and evaluating strategies under high uncertainty? It just isn't true. No one framework or tool is universally applicable.

Which specific tools and frameworks should business strategists use to supplement the traditional strategy toolkit? Chapter 6 and the appendix address this fundamental strategic-planning and decision-making question. Once again, the answer depends on the level of residual uncertainty facing the strategist. Decision analysis, for example, is particularly relevant when facing Level 2 uncertainty. Scenario planning, on the other hand, can help define possible future outcomes under Levels 2 and 3 uncertainty, but it is inappropriate for Level 1 issues.

Chapter 6 provides a brief overview of the relevant toolkit for each level of residual uncertainty, and the appendix provides more details on five of the most common tools. Together they provide a road map for identifying the right set of tools for making any given strategy decision under uncertainty. They do not, however, provide enough information to ensure that novice readers will become expert practitioners of each tool or framework. Therefore, the appendix provides a set of references for those interested in further study.

New Strategic-Planning and Decision-Making Processes?

Typical strategic-planning and decision-making processes run on an internal calendar cycle, repeating every one to five years. Key elements of the strategy are reviewed and updated during each cycle. But there is often a reluctance to make major changes, at least for a few years.

These processes can serve companies well in environments that are predictable. But these same processes are limited, and even dangerous, under Levels 2–4 uncertainty. Why? Because the standard planning cycle limits the ability of the company to change direction in response to—or in anticipation of—new opportunities or threats.

If typical strategic-planning and decision-making processes are inappropriate in highly uncertain business environments, what alternative processes should companies use to monitor and update their strategies over time? Chapter 7 addresses this question and offers three distinct approaches that companies can use to monitor, update, and even revise strategies in turbulent markets. Not surprisingly, the best approach for your company depends on the level of residual uncertainty it faces.

DEVELOPING YOUR OWN ANSWERS: SOME HINTS FOR USING THIS BOOK

As outlined above, this book is built around the five questions that business strategists, in my experience, find most vexing about strategy under high uncertainty. Most senior business decision makers, their consultants, and their staffs face these questions on an ongoing basis. They should find the book immediately applicable to their day-to-day activities and decision making. First and foremost, this book is written for them.

The book offers no one-size-fits-all answers to these fundamental strategy questions. However, there is a common framework—the four levels of residual uncertainty—which should help you achieve the foresight necessary to craft your own value-creating answers. This is primarily a "how to think about it" book, one that provides principles, frameworks, and examples to guide your own deliberations rather than bold, oversold prescriptions.

If you are an experienced business strategist, familiar with the prototypical strategy toolkit and increasingly frustrated by its inapplicability to many of today's strategy problems, then this book is for you. If you are new to business strategy, however, some prereading on basic strategy approaches and vocabulary might be a better place to start.[5]

This book is intended for strategists across a broad range of industries, from high-tech sectors like electronics, telecommunications, and biotechnology to industrial sectors like chemicals, transportation, and pulp and paper. The latter are often characterized as slow-moving, predictable sectors. However, McKinsey's consulting experience across a wide range of industries suggests that strategists in even these industries face crucial decisions that must be made under uncertainty, decisions that can't be adequately addressed using prototypical strategic-planning and decision-making processes. That's why the book features examples and principles derived from a variety of industry settings rather than focusing solely on currently "hot" sectors like e-commerce.[6]

The book not only helps senior executives think about uncertainty in new ways, but also gives consultants and strategic-planning staffs the "how to do it" knowledge they need. While the book does not provide detailed step-by-step instructions for completing staff work, it is organized around a four-step process for developing, monitoring, and updating strategies over time. This process is summarized in figure 1-1.

Step 1: Define the Strategic Issue and the Level of Residual Uncertainty

After clarifying the strategic issue at hand—for example, whether and how to enter a new market—strategy development under uncertainty should always start with an attempt to achieve 20/20 foresight around the factors that drive this choice. The unknown must be separated from the

Figure 1-1   Strategy under Uncertainty: Four-Step Process

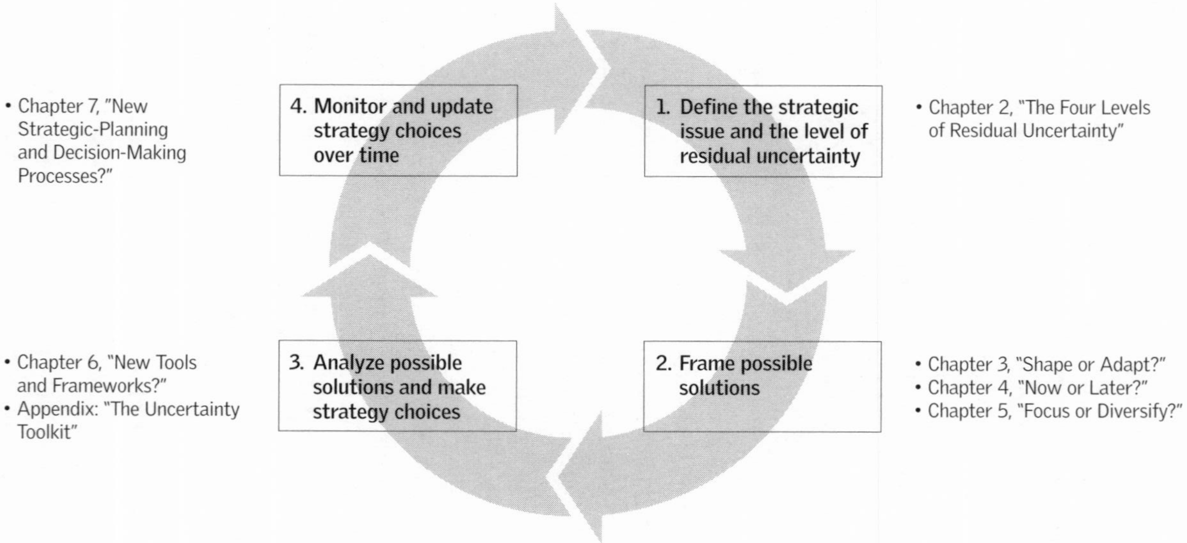

- Chapter 2, "The Four Levels of Residual Uncertainty"

1. Define the strategic issue and the level of residual uncertainty

2. Frame possible solutions

- Chapter 3, "Shape or Adapt?"
- Chapter 4, "Now or Later?"
- Chapter 5, "Focus or Diversify?"

4. Monitor and update strategy choices over time

3. Analyze possible solutions and make strategy choices

- Chapter 7, "New Strategic-Planning and Decision-Making Processes?"

- Chapter 6, "New Tools and Frameworks?"
- Appendix: "The Uncertainty Toolkit"

unknowable, identifying the level of residual uncertainty. Chapter 2 provides the framework for doing so.

Step 2: Frame Possible Solutions

Once the level of residual uncertainty is identified, strategists can begin framing and refining possible solutions. Knowing the level of uncertainty helps define feasible opportunities to shape or adapt, bet big today or stage commitments over time, or build a strategy that is robust to the range of possible outcomes. Chapters 3–5 address these fundamental choices and should help you frame possible solutions to your company's strategic issues.

Step 3: Analyze Possible Solutions and Make Strategy Choices

The analytical tools, frameworks, and decision-making models discussed in chapter 6 and the appendix allow you to tailor your approach to the level of uncertainty you face and make the right choices.

Step 4: Monitor and Update Strategy Choices over Time

Given the rapid pace of change in highly uncertain business environments, you will undoubtedly have to monitor and update strategy choices over time—in essence, repeating steps 1–3 over and over again. Chapter 7 identifies the systems and processes necessary to do this most effectively.

If you are interested in "how to do it," reading chapters 2–7 in sequence will take you through this four-step process. If you are interested in "how to think about it" instead, you should start with chapter 2, because understanding the material on the four levels of residual uncertainty is a prerequisite to effective use of the rest of the book. But you may then choose to read subsequent chapters in an order determined by your most pressing strategy interests and needs. For example, if you are certain you want to shape, but don't know whether to do it now or later, you might jump directly from chapter 2 to chapter 4. In any event, whether you bought this book seeking advice on "how to do" or "how to think about" strategy under uncertainty, it is organized in a way that should meet your needs.

Finally, while *20/20 Foresight* is a practitioner's book, it should also prove useful to business school academics and their M.B.A. students. As a supplementary text in required or advanced business strategy and policy courses, it will help students understand the need to tailor strategic analyses, choices, and ongoing management processes to the level of residual uncertainty. And for academics, it provides an integrating framework for classifying uncertainty and assessing the applicability of competing one-size-fits-all prescriptions to strategy under uncertainty.

CRAFTING STRATEGY IN AN UNCERTAIN WORLD

As you work through this book you won't walk away with any universally applicable approaches. But you will become equipped with a powerful arsenal of approaches that, with a little bit of work, can be tailored to your organization's core strategy issues. It may take a bit of time and effort to embed these approaches in your organizations, and the immediate return on this investment is unclear. But given the enormous upside to making the right strategy choices at the right time, this is one investment under uncertainty you can bank on.

2

THE FOUR LEVELS
OF RESIDUAL UNCERTAINTY

I F YOU WANT to understand the differences between strategy in reasonably certain and highly uncertain markets, consider the telecommunications industry. This sector has endured both predictable and
wildly unpredictable environments—and its executives have learned that
winning strategies must be tailored to the level of uncertainty.

For decades, the telecommunications industry was a regulated industry, meaning that its markets were secure, its returns guaranteed, and its
executives coddled in a world where risk was virtually unknown. Today,
however, that world has been turned upside down: Deregulation, the
breakup of former monopolies like AT&T, and the privatization of state-
owned companies like Deutsche Telekom have unleashed a flood of new
competitors and technological innovation. The rapid pace of change has
created uncertainty the likes of which most senior telecommunications
managers never imagined. With this uncertainty have come unprecedented opportunities and hazards.

Nowhere is this change more evident than in the broadband market.
The race is currently on between cable, telecommunications, and satellite companies to upgrade their infrastructures to provide high-speed,
interactive access for new video, voice, and data services in homes and

businesses. Entertainment, media, Internet, and traditional telecommunications companies are all competing to develop and market these services. Meanwhile, hardware and software providers are jockeying to establish their devices and programs as standards in this emerging industry.

All of this activity is taking place in an extremely uncertain, competitive environment. Everyone agrees that the demand for broadband services will be big—very big—one day. But it is still unclear which services and distribution channels consumers will prefer (and at what price), despite volumes of market research. Opinions differ, as well, over which technologies, which business models, and which regulatory frameworks will ultimately prevail in the broadband market.

Despite this uncertainty, there has been no shortage of bold strategic moves, including high-stakes acquisitions. AT&T spent over $100 billion on acquisitions to reach 25 percent of U.S. cable households as a means to provide end-to-end phone services as well as to secure broadband access to the home through cable modems. Microsoft cofounder and independent entrepreneur Paul Allen spent 1998 and 1999 acquiring $25 billion worth of cable and Internet companies as his broadband play. And in perhaps the boldest move of them all, America Online (AOL) merged with Time Warner.

These companies are betting big on what are clearly uncertain prospects. They have exposed themselves to potential massive losses. So why don't they postpone these big bets until they can be more confident about their returns? The answer is pretty obvious: The competitive landscape is so crowded and so fierce that companies that hesitate to make their move risk losing the broadband market altogether. This is the broadband decision maker's dilemma: Bet big and you may win big or lose big. Don't bet at all and you may lose the opportunity to play in any future games.

How do companies decide to take the risk? And, more important, how *should* they decide? The following story may shed some light on this question. In the early 1990s—long before the emergence of the World Wide Web and thus the desire for high-speed Internet access— executives at a company I'll call Alpha Telecommunications were attempting to formulate a broadband strategy. Alpha was the incumbent provider of local telephone services in a large U.S. region.[1]

Cable television companies were already upgrading their networks to carry interactive content, and Alpha believed that pending deregulation would allow them to offer local telephone service as an inexpensive add-on to their rich entertainment offerings. With such an attractive product bundle, the cable companies might capture a large share of Alpha's existing telephone revenue. At the same time, these companies would capture the lion's share of new revenues from broadband entertainment content. Alpha's executives worried that unless it could offer a competitive product bundle, its revenue growth might be severely curtailed.

If Alpha wanted to offer broadband services, it would have to upgrade its telephone network.[2] But this wouldn't come cheap. It would cost several billion dollars to upgrade the network using the most attractive broadband technology available at the time. An investment of this magnitude could only be justified if it resulted in a significantly higher retained market share in local telephone service, produced a large stream of revenues from new entertainment and information services, and substantially lowered network maintenance costs.

To help clarify its network development choice, Alpha turned to its strategic-planning and decision-making toolkit. Like many companies, Alpha's toolkit was designed to conduct thorough industry analyses that specified the relative attractiveness of different markets, and identified Alpha's potential sources of competitive advantage. Porter's Five Forces framework provided the checklist for Alpha's assessment of the broadband industry.

While this framework posed all the right questions, Alpha found that analysis of the current telecommunications and cable industries did not offer precise answers. For example, the regulatory framework for local telephone competition was still under debate, making it unclear who would enter the market, when they would do it, and what their entry strategies would be. At the same time, the latent demand for broadband services—many of which had not even been conceived yet, let alone developed and marketed—was highly uncertain. Nor was it clear which network technologies, brands, or relationships with content providers would prove to be sources of sustainable competitive advantage in the broadband market. In short, an industry analysis built around the Five Forces framework would provide insight on the current state of the telecommunications and cable industries, but precious little foresight on the future state of the nascent broadband market. And such foresight was the key to making the right broadband network investment choice.

BINARY VIEWS OF UNCERTAINTY

Each of Alpha's key value drivers in making the right investment choice—which included retained local telephone market share (in a market that was not yet competitive), network operating cost savings (for a technology that had not been fully tested), and revenue streams (from new entertainment services that had not yet been conceived)—was highly uncertain. This uncertainty dominated Alpha's deliberations. What was the best way to proceed given the magnitude of the bet? Here's a paraphrased exchange that transpired among Alpha's senior managers:

> *Manager 1:* I know in my gut this is going to work. Don't worry if we don't have the data to support it. Let's make this bet.
> *Manager 2:* But we don't know anything for sure. Let's stick to what we do know, and focus instead on reengineering our current businesses.
> *Manager 3:* It doesn't matter what we know at this point. Everyone else is moving on broadband, and we have to, too, if we want to remain competitive.

Despite their different viewpoints, all three were making a common mistake: treating uncertainty as an all-or-nothing, black-and-white proposition—the so-called binary view of uncertainty that was defined in chapter 1. Faced with an "uncertain" problem, these managers were leaning more heavily on intuition, "collective wisdom," and personal-risk tolerance rather than on the rigorous decision-making tools and processes they so religiously applied to more "certain" problems in their core business.

To Alpha's credit, it realized that multi-billion-dollar investment decisions—to the extent possible—should not be made without the facts. To help forecast consumer demand for broadband services, Alpha had hired two firms to undertake market research studies. Both firms were leaders in their field, and both came back with fundamentally different answers. One study forecasted demand-levels that implied a 25 percent return on investment (ROI) on the broadband network, while the other suggested a significant loss!

At this point, many discussions centered around which estimate was "right." Alpha was now exhibiting the other side of the binary mind-set trap. In initial discussions, it had assumed that broadband service demand was "uncertain" and could not be analyzed. Now it had gone to the opposite extreme of assuming that the right market research could identify a reliable point forecast. The problem with this line of thinking, however, was that neither of the studies was right or wrong. Rather, their range of estimates reflected real uncertainty in the marketplace about these yet-to-be-developed broadband services.

FROM BINARY UNCERTAINTY
TO RESIDUAL UNCERTAINTY

So what was this uncertainty that remained after the two market research studies? As I've mentioned earlier, I call it residual uncertainty. Residual uncertainty is the uncertainty left over after the best possible analysis of the problem at hand. Residual uncertainty is not what you *don't* know—it's what you *can't* know.

Decision makers achieve 20/20 foresight when they accurately identify the residual uncertainty they face. Given the strategic issue at hand, they have developed the most accurate view of the future possible.

Using 20/20 foresight was the key to breaking the decision-making gridlock at Alpha. Analysis provided useful predictions of some key variables while bounding the range of outcomes on others. For example, the company began to study the business challenges that a cable provider would encounter in the local telephone business. This study concluded that cable companies would not achieve large near-term market shares in local telephone services. This analysis provided huge strategic insight to Alpha. Despite the long lead times involved in network build outs, Alpha did not need to make immediate full-scale commitments to new, broadband networks to protect itself from cable entry.

Alpha's market research studies, while only bounding the range of future broadband demand, also provided strategic insight. The optimistic demand scenario was so positive that it convinced Alpha that it had to stay in the broadband game. But the pessimistic demand scenario also clarified the risk in embarking upon an immediate full-scale network build out.

With this fresh understanding, Alpha launched a series of small-scale broadband service experiments. Such experiments would keep Alpha in the game, but postpone major network build-out decisions until these early experiments generated better data on network economics. This experimental approach would also free up capital for more immediate competitive threats to its existing network, including wireless competition and the entry of competitive local exchange carriers.

If Alpha had held to a binary view, rather than embracing the concept of residual uncertainty, it would not have arrived at this experiment-based strategy. Instead, managers would have continued to argue over which market research study was right, aligning themselves with the estimate that confirmed their original hunches. Managers 1 and 3 would have argued that the optimistic demand estimate was correct, while manager 2 would have extolled the virtues of the pessimistic estimate. Eventually, one side would have prevailed, with the most likely result being either a full-scale network build out or no broadband investment at all. This is the trap of an all-or-nothing view of uncertainty: It drives managers toward all-or-nothing strategy choices. Strategists with 20/20 foresight, on the other hand, often identify staged, partial-commitment strategies that manage downside risk while maintaining upside opportunities.

TOWARD 20/20 FORESIGHT:
THE FOUR LEVELS OF RESIDUAL UNCERTAINTY

As the Alpha case illustrates, residual uncertainty, not binary uncertainty, is the way to frame strategic decisions in today's rapidly changing, uncertain economy. But how can decision makers effectively move from mind-set to practice?

For any given decision, they must first identify the variables that matter in crafting the right strategy. Typically, this includes customer demand (at different product-price combinations), drivers of capital and operating costs, technology performance, competitor behavior, and even regulatory and legislative outcomes. They must also identify the relevant time frame to use in evaluating strategy choices. When a pharmaceutical company is deciding whether to develop a new drug, for example, the time frame of the patent is considered. The cash flows during this time frame will determine whether its strategy is successful or not.

Next, decision makers must ask themselves what is—or can be (with the right analysis)—known about these key variables over this time frame. Their answers always take one of four general forms:

1. A clear, single view of the future

2. A limited set of possible future outcomes, one of which will occur

3. A range of possible future outcomes

4. A limitless range of possible future outcomes

These four, in fact, define the four levels of residual uncertainty (as summarized in figure 2-1).[3] Summaries and examples of each of the four levels of uncertainty are highlighted in tables 2-1 through 2-4 and in the remainder of this section. Bookmark these pages! Understanding the level of residual uncertainty you face is essential to achieving 20/20 foresight and crafting winning strategies under uncertainty.

Level 1: A Clear Enough Future

Strategists facing Level 1 uncertainty have a clear, single view of the future. This is not to say that all potential drivers of their strategy choices are 100 percent predictable.

I can't think of any important decision I have faced in my life—or in my clients' lives—where the outcome was completely predictable. But I have faced plenty of choices where the outcome was predictable enough to identify a clear, confident decision. For example, I recently purchased a house in suburban Maryland. The house's likely resale value at different points in the future was a key driver of my buying decision. The real estate market in my neighborhood was stable and predictable enough to allow me, with a little research, to generate clear point forecasts of future resale values. I realized that these point forecasts wouldn't be completely on target, yet I was confident that they would be close enough to reality that this uncertainty didn't affect my decision to buy the house. The resale value of the house, then, was a Level 1 uncertainty.

Likewise, business strategists face Level 1 uncertainty when they face opportunities where the range of possible future outcomes is narrow enough that this uncertainty doesn't matter, in terms of making a decision. Indeed, under Level 1 uncertainty, strategists can develop point forecasts that are precise enough for strategy development.

Alpha faced some Level 1 uncertainties, for example, when it formulated its broadband network investment strategy. Reasonably precise forecasts were available for cable penetration rates into local telephone

Figure 2-1   The Four Levels of Residual Uncertainty

Strategists with 20/20 foresight can identify . . .

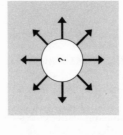

1   A clear enough future

A single view of the future

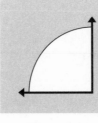

2   Alternate futures

A limited set of possible future outcomes, one of which will occur

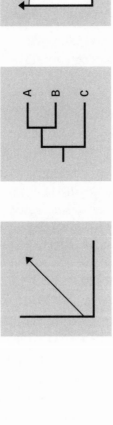

3   A range of futures

A range of possible future outcomes

4   True ambiguity

Not even a range of possible future outcomes

service over the next three to five years, as were capital cost estimates for broadband network build outs. The ranges of possible future outcomes for these two variables were narrow enough that this uncertainty did not affect Alpha's network investment decision.

Pure Level 1 situations—in which the future path of every key value driver is clear enough—are increasingly uncommon in today's economy. Pure Level 1 situations usually occur in well-established markets that are not prone to external shocks or internal upheaval. They tend to be in industries with stable regulatory and legislative structures, in lower-tech markets with incremental innovation rates, and in industries with relatively high entry barriers that limit new entrants, competition from incumbents, and great changes in the purchasing behavior of customers.

McDonald's generally faces Level 1 uncertainty when it decides where to locate its new U.S. restaurants. By studying customer demographics, traffic flows, real estate availability and prices, and locations of competitive outlets, McDonald's can forecast a new restaurant's earnings. Although the forecasts aren't perfect, they are close enough to make a confident yes-no decision on any potential restaurant location.

Information-rich, slow-moving environments—such as the fast-food industry—are where most Level 1 strategy issues are found. Many retail industries share these traits. As a result, when established retailers like Wal-Mart or The Home Depot make their own U.S. store location decisions, they, too, likely face Level 1 uncertainty.

The pricing, marketing, and product or service features decisions for well-established brands are also often made under Level 1 uncertainty. Suppose Toyota wants to reposition the Camry versus the Honda Accord in the U.S. auto market. Since the family sedan is a well-defined product category with relatively stable brand positions, Toyota's market research would enable it to generate reasonably precise forecasts of the effects of any new pricing or marketing strategies. It is unlikely that Toyota would face residual uncertainty in this case that would prevent it from making a clear, confident strategy choice.

Even strategy choices that look like big bets may, in fact, be made under Level 1 uncertainty. When British Petroleum (now BP) acquired Amoco, it certainly faced uncertainty over future oil prices and post-merger integration synergies. Yet the acquisition was heralded as a sure thing by many industry observers. Why? One possibility is that the range of future outcomes defined by these residual uncertainties wasn't wide enough—in particular, the downside wasn't severe enough—to call the acquisition decision into question. In other words, these were Level 1 residual uncertainties for British Petroleum when it came to making its Amoco acquisition decision.

Using similar logic, it follows that even new business entry and market exit decisions may be made under Level 1 uncertainty. When Huntsman Chemical acquired Imperial Chemical Industries' (ICI's) plants and entered the titanium dioxide business in 1999, it made this decision under Level 1 uncertainty.[4] Huntsman was acquiring an existing player in an industry with relatively stable structure and conduct, and it thus could generate a forecast of future cash flows that was clear enough to make a confident decision.

The examples of Level 1 uncertainty just discussed are summarized in table 2-1.

Level 2: Alternate Futures

To understand Level 2 uncertainty, think back to all those true-false and multiple-choice exams you took in school. If you're like me, you faced many questions where you just didn't know the answer. But the nice thing about these exams was that you always had a *chance* of being right:

Table 2-1   Sources of Level 1 Uncertainty: Examples

Source of Uncertainty	Example Decisions	Specific Level 1 Uncertainties
• Returns on "common" investments in mature, stable markets	• U.S. restaurant locations for McDonald's; U.S. retail store locations for The Home Depot	• Customer demand and cost parameters in a stable market environment with relatively stable business models and reliable information sources
• Customer and competitor reactions to strategies that reposition well-established brands	• U.S. marketing and pricing strategy for the Toyota Camry	• Customer response and competitive response from brands such as the Honda Accord in the well-established and well-understood family sedan market
• Returns on "uncommon" investments in mature, stable markets	• British Petroleum's acquisition of competitor Amoco	• Postmerger integration synergies and other drivers of acquisition value
	• Huntsman Chemical's entry into the titanium dioxide business	• Value of ICI's business in the relatively stable titanium dioxide business

Each question had a limited set of possible answers, one of which was correct. The answer was always true or false (or, in multiple-choice questions, it was limited to A, B, C, or D). This set of possible answers was always mutually exclusive and collectively exhaustive (or MECE in the language of McKinsey consultants). MECE implies that one, and only one, of these possible answers was correct.

Similarly, strategists facing Level 2 uncertainty can identify a MECE set of possible future outcomes, one of which will occur. Analysis, although it may help establish relative probabilities, cannot tell you which one will occur (as it could under Level 1 uncertainty). This matters because the best strategy to follow depends on which outcome ultimately occurs.

Investors in the U.S. stock market, for instance, faced Level 2 uncertainty in trying to determine the identity of the next president of the United States throughout the fall of 2000. Investors knew that the next president would be either George W. Bush or Al Gore, but on election day, and even weeks later, no one could say for sure who had won. This uncertainty mattered to investors since the candidates proposed policies that might have opposite effects on the profits—and thus share prices—of companies in certain industries. For example, it was thought that health insurance stocks would benefit from a Bush victory.

Potential regulatory, legislative, or judicial changes are often sources of Level 2 uncertainty—since it is often possible to identify a MECE set of possible outcomes ahead of time. How and when will regulatory or legislative reforms be enacted? Often, there is a limited set of clear possibilities. There seem to be a limited number of models that the regulation or deregulation of public utilities can take, for example, just as there are only a limited number of politically feasible environmental legislation changes at any given time in any given country.

Many U.S. health maintenance organizations (HMOs) faced Level 2 legislative uncertainty when they were deciding whether to offer managed care products to Medicaid recipients in the mid-1990s. The Medicaid business was not expected to be very profitable on a stand-alone basis. High profits would encourage competitors to enter the market. At the same time, the government would likely cut back on its reimbursement rates to HMOs; after all, the average taxpayer is not interested in subsidizing HMO profits. Both factors would tend to check potential HMO profits in the Medicaid market.

As a result, HMOs often focused on the impact their entry into the Medicaid market would have on the profitability of their *other* product lines when formulating their Medicaid strategies. For example, many HMOs feared that state legislatures would mandate that only those HMOs that offered Medicaid products would be allowed to contract with the state to serve relatively healthy (and thus more profitable) groups of state employees.

This created an important Level 2 uncertainty: Would HMOs be required to offer a Medicaid product in order to qualify to bid for other state contracts? This question had only two possible answers—yes or no. As many HMOs formulated their Medicaid strategies, whether the answer was going to be yes or no was unclear, yet it was a key determinant of their entry decisions.

Uncertainty over future regulatory changes in California is creating Level 2 uncertainty for independent power producers (IPPs) considering building power plants in the state. California was one of the first states to deregulate its electric power markets. However, the results to date have been largely disappointing. For example, fundamental supply-demand imbalances caused electricity prices in San Diego to rise 200 to 300 percent during the summer of 2000, and rolling blackouts were experienced across the state in early 2001. These and similar high-profile market failures are creating political pressure to "rederegulate" (or even "reregulate") the California market. There is a MECE set of models the state could choose from to change electric power regulations. IPPs can identify these models and the implications each would have on power producers in the state; they just don't know which one (if any) will be implemented.

Unpredictable competitor moves and countermoves are also often sources of Level 2 uncertainty. Will one of my competitors build a new plant? License a technology? Attempt to acquire a third party? Will a new competitor enter this market? All are questions with a MECE set of possible answers that can be identified ahead of time. What often can't be identified ahead of time, however, is which one of these possible actions your competitor will actually choose.

When Georgia-Pacific (GP) makes decisions to expand its papermaking capacity, for example, it often faces Level 2 uncertainty over the capacity-expansion plans of competitors like International Paper. Since GP understands the economics of paper plant investments (i.e., to the extent it is familiar with competitor operations), it can identify a limited set of feasible capacity-expansion projects for its competitors at any given time. But it may not be able to predict with certainty which projects, if any, its competitors will pick. And these competitor choices matter to GP in formulating its own strategy. If all producers bring on new capacity at the same time, the sudden excess in supply will cause prices to fall and make it difficult to earn an adequate return on investment.

In the summer of 2000, analysts suggested that French megaretailer Carrefour was a likely acquisition candidate for Wal-Mart. Wal-Mart had signaled its intent to grow internationally and Carrefour held coveted positions in Europe and emerging markets where Wal-Mart was currently underrepresented. Besides, Carrefour's share price had recently tanked, making it a more feasible Wal-Mart takeover target. Carrefour could not know for sure, however, whether Wal-Mart would try to acquire it or otherwise enter the French market. This Level 2 uncertainty mattered, because if Carrefour was certain that Wal-Mart would attempt a takeover, it might favor a preemptive U.S. acquisition of its own. Carrefour might then be "too big"—both in terms of acquisition costs and antitrust implications—for Wal-Mart to swallow. Without the Wal-Mart takeover threat, however, Carrefour might continue to focus on growth outside the United States.[5]

All-or-nothing industry standards competition is also a common source of Level 2 uncertainty. Some products are more valuable to a given consumer the more other consumers already use the product. An example is the telephone. The more people own telephones, the more valuable my own telephone is. This is also true for certain technology standards that facilitate communication, transactions, or other interactions between and among consumers and businesses. For example, the more people use a given computer operating system like Windows, the more valuable Windows is to me since it makes it more likely that I will be able to easily communicate and share information with other computer users.

Whenever the utility one gets from a product is dependent on others using the product, we have what economists call *network externalities.* Positive network externalities—I like Windows more if you use it, and you like Windows more if I use it—can create all-or-nothing market share wars where one product or one standard will eventually replace all others. That's why we all use VHS instead of Beta videocassette recorders (VCRs).

Before the winning standard emerges, however, strategists often face Level 2 uncertainty. In the early VCR market, for example, it was clear that either VHS or Beta would become the industry standard—but it wasn't clear which one. Similarly, personal computer software developers in the late 1980s faced Level 2 uncertainty over which operating system standard—DOS, OS/2, Macintosh, Windows, or Unix—would emerge as the next-generation industry standard. This uncertainty mattered because it forced developers to either bet on one standard versus another, or hedge their bets by developing programs for different operating system platforms.

Likewise, when Circuit City formulated its Divx digital videodisk strategy, it faced Level 2 uncertainty around whether it would be able to displace the established DVD standard. Similarly, QUALCOMM faced Level 2 uncertainty as it tried to establish its code division multiple access (CDMA) technology as the unified standard for third-generation (3G) wireless phones and networks. Other technologies, like time division multiple access (TDMA) and global system for mobile communications (GSM) (the dominant U.S. and European standards, respectively, in earlier generations), were also competing to become *the* standard adopted by wireless telephone manufacturers. Ultimately, Divx failed and CDMA won. But in both cases, strategists faced all-or-nothing, Level 2 uncertainty when formulating their market entry, licensing, marketing, and pricing strategies.[6] Table 2-2 summarizes the examples of Level 2 uncertainty just presented.

Table 2-2   Sources of Level 2 Uncertainty: Examples

Source of Uncertainty	Example Decisions	Specific Level 2 Uncertainties
• Potential regulatory, legislative, or judicial changes	• HMOs' strategies to enter the Medicaid HMO market	• Whether states would require HMOs to offer Medicaid products if they wanted to bid for other state contracts
	• Independent power producer's decision to build power plants in California	• Future changes in the regulatory environment caused by early deregulation failures
• Unpredictable competitor moves and countermoves	• GP's decision to add new papermaking capacity	• Competitor capacity-expansion plans
	• Carrefour's U.S. entry strategy	• Whether Wal-Mart was going to attempt to acquire Carrefour
• All-or-nothing industry standards competition	• Personal computer software developer's choice of which operating systems to develop software for in the late 1980s	• Which operating system would become the industry standard
	• Circuit City's Divx strategy	• Which platform—Divx or DVD—would become the digital videodisk industry standard
	• QUALCOMM's chip development strategy	• Which technology—TDMA, GSM, or CDMA—would become the industry standard in wireless phones and networks

Level 3: A Range of Futures

In some respects, Level 3 uncertainty is like Level 2 uncertainty: One can identify the range of possible future outcomes, but no obvious point forecast emerges. And in both cases, this range is wide enough to matter when making strategy decisions. But there is a very important difference: Strategists facing Level 3 uncertainty can only define a *representative* set of outcomes within the range of possible outcomes. Unlike Level 2 situations, this set will not be MECE. The outcomes will merely be representative of what might occur, and thus not collectively exhaustive. Some other point within the range of possible outcomes could very well occur.

To illustrate this difference, reconsider the market research studies that Alpha commissioned on broadband demand. The studies identified two possible outcomes: one that would generate a 25 percent ROI for Alpha, and another that would result in a substantial loss. Was this set of outcomes MECE? No. The set identified the range of possible outcomes, but any point within this range—say a 10 percent ROI—was also possible. Alpha faced Level 3, not Level 2, uncertainty around broadband demand.

On the other hand, investors in the stock market *could* identify a MECE set of outcomes to the U.S. presidential election in 2000: Either Bush or Gore would win. These weren't representative outcomes. They were the *only* possible outcomes. Investors faced Level 2, not Level 3, uncertainty over the U.S. election results.

As in the Alpha case, customer demand for new products and services is a common source of Level 3 uncertainty. Market research, experiments, pilots, and analogies from similar situations often provide useful information on the latent demand for such products, but they rarely generate reliable point forecasts. Rather, they usually generate a range of outcomes that inform decision making but do not identify any obvious strategic direction.

This is the issue that Airbus faces in making its decision to launch a new "superjumbo" jet, the A380. Airbus research suggests that the market for jumbo and superjumbo planes may be as large as 1,500 units over the next twenty years. Boeing, on the other hand, projects that the market might be as small as 350 planes over the same period. The actual market size might be anywhere in between. And exactly where it falls within this range matters. Lehman Brothers, for example, projects that Airbus would have to sell 528 superjumbos over the next twenty years just to break even.[7]

Enron also faces Level 3 uncertainty over customer demand as it attempts to build its new bandwidth-trading business. As it has done with other commodities—most notably natural gas and electricity—Enron is attempting to build a liquid market where excess bandwidth can be bought and sold. However, there is significant uncertainty over suppliers' willingness to sell excess bandwidth and potential customers' desire to contract for bandwidth in smaller, time-of-day increments. This implies a very broad range of estimates for the volume of bandwidth trades that will be executed by Enron's market makers. This range matters: If trade demand is weak enough, Enron won't be able to recover its market development costs.[8]

Like Enron, companies launching new products and services often confront uncertainty over the performance and customer acceptance of their new, competing technologies, business models, or processes relative to alternatives. These companies face uncertainty over the size of the new economic pie *and* the size of their slice.

As the broadband market develops, customers will be able to choose from cable modem, DSL, satellite, and fixed-wireless modes to access content. Companies building the infrastructures to provide broadband service have to worry about total broadband demand growth as well as how this demand will break out between competing access technologies. They face Level 3 uncertainty when making such infrastructure investment choices: Only broad ranges of demand estimates by access technology are reliable. AT&T, for example, faced Level 3 uncertainty when it spent $100 billion to acquire Tele-Communications, Inc. and MediaOne Group.

Similarly, Iridium faced Level 3 uncertainty when it launched its $5 billion satellite telephone network. It faced uncertainty not only over the growth in mobile telephone demand in total, but also over the share that satellite telephone service would be able to capture relative to the rapidly expanding and improving set of cellular alternatives. Again, only a wide range of estimates was feasible as Iridium launched its satellites. This is exactly the type of uncertainty automakers face as they pour research and development (R&D) dollars into fuel cell and hybrid (combining gas and electric power sources) alternatives to gas-powered vehicles.[9] The cost and performance attributes of these alternatives are uncertain enough that reliable point forecasts of consumer demand are impossible to obtain. However, this is not a Level 4 situation where one cannot even bound the range of possible outcomes.

Finally, unstable macroeconomic conditions—creating unpredictable gross domestic product (GDP) growth, inflation and interest rates, and currency fluctuations—are another common source of Level 3 uncertainty. In some cases, the range of potential outcomes doesn't matter for strategic decision making (suggesting it is a Level 1 variable). For example, the range of estimates on U.S. GDP growth over the next five to ten years shouldn't affect BellSouth's U.S. broadband strategies today. However, the range of estimates on Argentina's GDP growth may indeed be wide enough to influence the telecommunications infrastructure strategies BellSouth's subsidiary Movicom BellSouth, pursues in Argentina over the next few years. Macroeconomic instability in Argentina in late 2000 is great enough to create Level 3 uncertainty over the growth rate of demand for new telecommunications services.

Similarly, when Heineken entered a joint venture with South African Breweries to import and market its beer in South Africa in 1998, and as other consumer goods companies enter the Russian market today, they face Level 3 demand uncertainty driven by macroeconomic factors. Macroeconomic uncertainty allows for only a broad range of forecasts for personal income growth and distribution—and thus a broad range of demand estimates for consumer goods (especially luxury goods). Some of the many examples of Level 3 uncertainty are summarized in table 2-3.

Table 2-3   Sources of Level 3 Uncertainty: Examples

Source of Uncertainty	Example Decisions	Specific Level 3 Uncertainties
• Customer demand for new products or services	• Airbus's commitment to build the A380	• Demand for superjumbo-jets
	• Enron's bandwidth-trading strategy	• Demand for bandwidth trades through Enron's market makers
• The relative performance of and customer preference for new, competing technologies, business models, or processes	• AT&T's cable acquisitions	• Cable's penetration rate in broadband markets relative to alternatives
	• Iridium's satellite telephone investments	• Relative performance, and thus demand for, satellite telephones versus alternatives
	• Automakers' investments in fuel cell and hybrid cars	• Relative performance, and thus demand for, these "greener" alternatives versus traditional models
• Unstable macroeconomic conditions	• Movicom BellSouth's telecommunications infrastructure investments in Argentina	• Personal income growth and distribution in Argentina
	• Heineken's entry into the South African beer market	• Personal income growth and distribution in South Africa
	• Consumer goods company's Russian entry strategy	• Personal income growth and distribution in Russia

Level 4: True Ambiguity

Future outcomes for Level 4 uncertainties are both unknown—*and unknowable.* Analysis cannot even identify the range of potential future outcomes, let alone scenarios within that range. As far as the strategist can tell, there is a limitless range of possible future outcomes. In fact, it might not even be possible to identify all the relevant variables that will define the future.

Level 4 situations are rare, and they tend to degrade over time to lower levels of uncertainty. Frequently, they occur in markets during and immediately after major technological, economic, or social discontinuities, as well as in markets that are just beginning to form. In either case, the entire future structure, conduct, and performance of the market are in question. Disruptions—such as a public backlash against genetically modified foods or a marketing coup by an e-commerce pioneer—could easily send the market spinning in a new direction. Anyone who imagines they can put bounds on the range of potential outcomes in such uncertain markets is engaging in wishful thinking.

Those considering major investments to enter the Russian market in the early 1990s faced Level 4 uncertainty. Such companies could not predict the laws and regulations that would govern property rights and transactions. That uncertainty was compounded by additional uncertainty over the viability of supply chains and the demand for previously unavailable consumer goods and services. Wild cards like political assassination or currency default could quickly undo ongoing political and economic reforms. These same sources of Level 4 uncertainty were evident for companies entering South Africa in the immediate postapartheid era. In either case, it was impossible to generate fact-based assessments of the upside and downside values of proposed entry strategies.

The same lack of clarity on almost all elements of industry structure, conduct, and performance can be seen in markets that are just beginning to form. Celera Genomics, for example, is a pioneer in the field of comparative genomics—the study of similar genes in different species. Celera intends to decode the genomes of several species over the next few years. Any cross-species similarities it finds may lead to unprecedented research and commercial opportunities. For example, Celera recently identified 177 fly genes that are similar to human genes linked with diseases like cancer and diabetes. By studying and manipulating the fly genes, Celera hopes to learn more about how these genes might be manipulated in humans, and as a result discover breakthrough gene therapies. As Celera crafts its comparative genomics strategy, it is impossible to bound the range of potential future outcomes. The scientific and business implications of its approach will only begin to clarify themselves over time.[10]

Similarly, e-commerce strategists faced Level 4 uncertainty a few years ago. The boundaries of the playing field were yet to be determined. The players and their strategies were not known. Would e-commerce transactions occur over proprietary or open networks? What payment and security standards would emerge? What would consumers buy online? What role would the government play in regulating transactions? What strategies would new entrants employ, and how would incumbent retailers and wholesalers respond? While one could imagine alternative scenarios, no one could be confident they had bound the range of potential outcomes. The same could be said today for players like Nokia and NTT DoCoMo that are trying to shape the emerging "m-commerce" industry (Internet access and all it entails, including e-commerce, via mobile phones).

Finally, some strategists face Level 4 uncertainty because the time frames for evaluating their strategies are so long that there is no basis to cap the range of potential future outcomes. When Royal Dutch/Shell began formulating its renewable energy strategy—solar, wind, and biomass (burning wood and other renewable resources) power—in the mid-1990s, it considered energy supply and demand conditions out to 2060! No confident bound could be put on these parameters more than sixty years into the future.[11] Table 2-4 summarizes these examples of "truly ambiguous" (Level 4) business situations.

Table 2-4   Sources of Level 4 Uncertainty: Examples

Source of Uncertainty	Example Decisions	Specific Level 4 Uncertainties
• The outcomes of major technological, economic, or social discontinuities	• Entry into Russia in 1992; entry into South Africa in the immediate post-apartheid era	• Extreme ambiguity over likely legal and market institutions, as well as over fundamental supply and demand drivers
• Market evolution in markets that are just beginning to form	• Celera Genomics's comparative genomics strategy • Early e-commerce investments • Nokia's m-commerce strategy	• The commercial implications of ongoing scientific discoveries • The commercial implications of the emergence of the Internet as a communications/interactions network • Long-term demand-and-supply conditions in the m-commerce industry
• Extraordinarily long time frames required to evaluate potential strategies	• Royal Dutch/Shell's long-term renewable energy strategy	• Alternative energy demand-and-supply conditions over a sixty-year period

WHAT LEVEL DO YOU FACE?

The previous section, figure 2-1, and tables 2-1 through 2-4 summarize the key attributes, and provide numerous examples of, each level of residual uncertainty. This material should help you identify the level you face or your company faces for any given strategic decision. When doing so, keep in mind the following four rules.

The Level of Residual Uncertainty Is Usually Determined by the Interaction of Multiple Uncertainties

Although it is useful to define the level of uncertainty around individual value drivers, like demand or cost performance, your primary concern should be the residual uncertainty over the possible *combinations* of these value drivers. After all, when assessing a business strategy, what matters most is the impact on the bottom line; what happens to individual drivers of the bottom line is usually less important.

When making its broadband investment decision, Alpha, for example, faced Level 1 uncertainty (near-term cable penetration rates into local telephone service), Level 2 uncertainty (pending outcomes of telecommunications deregulation legislation), and Level 3 uncertainty (broadband service demand). The uncertainty over these different value drivers combined to generate a broad range of ROI estimates for Alpha's proposed network investment. In making its investment decision, it was this range of bottom-line ROI estimates that determined the strategic uncertainty that Alpha faced. There was no MECE set of scenarios within this range (not Level 2), and the range was not narrow enough to support an obvious decision to build the network or not (not Level 1). Alpha faced Level 3 uncertainty when formulating its broadband network investment strategy.

Most Strategy Decisions Face Level 2 or Level 3 Uncertainty

While those with a binary view of uncertainty perceive mainly Level 1 and Level 4 issues, my experience across a broad range of low- and high-tech industries suggests that the vast majority of business strategy decisions are made under either Level 2 or Level 3 uncertainty. Decision makers can usually at least bound the range of potential outcomes, but they can rarely generate reliable point forecasts. Consequently, this book concentrates on strategy under Levels 2 and 3 uncertainty. These are the decisions where doing strategic analysis right is the hardest (you can't rely on the traditional strategy toolkit) yet most insightful (if you do the analysis right, you'll bound the uncertainty and develop 20/20 foresight). And these are the situations where companies often have the greatest opportunities to shape industry environments to their competitive advantage.

Time Influences the Level of Residual Uncertainty

Uncertainty is a time-sensitive phenomenon. Most uncertainties will eventually resolve themselves. A decade or so ago, Alpha's broadband investment strategy decision would have faced Level 4 uncertainty: No one could have even bound its market potential. But over time, more information became available on network costs, network performance attributes, potential applications, competitor strategies, and other important drivers of the broadband market. By the early to mid-1990s, it was a Level 3 problem. Eventually, anyone contemplating building a broadband network will be able to generate reasonably precise forecasts of investment returns—signifying a Level 1 issue.

In today's rapidly changing economy, there will always be "shocks" that create new sources of uncertainty. Yet absent such shocks, any strategic decision will tend to migrate toward lower levels of uncertainty over time. As in the Alpha case, time provides information that narrows the range of plausible future outcomes. A consumer goods company may face Level 3 uncertainty around demand for its products in an emerging market today. But with enough time, the company can learn more about demand by tracking the success of rival entrants, conducting and updating market research, and so on. Eventually, it will face Level 1 uncertainty around the decision to enter this market. Likewise, a basic materials company, in trying to determine its own expansion plans, may face Level 2 uncertainty stemming from uncertainty about the expansion plans of rivals. Eventually, the competitors' expansion plans will be revealed, and the company will face Level 1 uncertainty.

The time element in uncertainty is a key insight. It often makes sense to postpone major commitments until lower levels of residual uncertainty arrive. But not always: Sometimes the only way to capture first-mover advantages and become a market leader is to make such commitments despite high levels of residual uncertainty. Chapter 4 will discuss the optimal timing of strategic commitments in greater detail.

As noted earlier, choosing the right time frame for *evaluating* decisions is also important. McDonald's, for instance, faces enormous uncertainty around the structure, conduct, and performance of the fast-food industry twenty-five years from now. Such uncertainty, however, doesn't affect franchise location decisions today (which turn on cash flows generated in the next three to ten years), and so McDonald's needn't be overly concerned. On the other hand, companies in industries with capital-intensive, long-payback projects (such as Alpha's broadband investment) require longer evaluation horizons (usually translating into higher levels of residual uncertainty).

The Level of Residual Uncertainty
Is Issue- and Company-Specific, Not Industry-Specific

There is no such thing as a "Level 3 industry." Levels of uncertainty rise and fall depending on the particular decision being made. For example, McDonald's executives face Level 1 uncertainty when making franchise location decisions in the United States. However, when launching a new product (like the failed McLean Deluxe sandwich), or entering new markets (like China), McDonald's faces Level 3 uncertainty—because for these products and markets McDonald's can only forecast broad ranges of potential sales. And these ranges matter for formulating the right market entry or product launch strategy. Likewise, Alpha faced Level 3 uncertainty when formulating its broadband strategy and Level 1 uncertainty when deciding its local-market telephone pricing strategy in the mid-1990s.

Recognizing that uncertainty is issue-specific—not industry-specific—is very important. Managers all too often view their industries as having "high" or "low" uncertainty, and so they adopt a one-size-fits-all approach to strategic decision making.

This can be dangerous. Many chemical companies, for example, consider themselves in relatively low-uncertainty environments. Thus, they have developed a set of decision-making processes that require precise forecasts and ROI calculations for any strategic decision. These processes tend to work quite well when making decisions around capacity, sales, marketing, and development of existing technologies and products. But any chemical company, at least one intent on surviving, makes a number of strategic decisions each year on new product or process development, commercialization, and market entry or exit that are not amenable to precise forecasts and investment return calculations.

Likewise, companies in such high-tech industries as computers, e-commerce, and telecommunications tend to think of themselves as competing in high-uncertainty industries. Strategic decision-making processes in these industries tend to be biased more toward action and experimentation, and less toward the traditional business case strategic-planning approach.[12] But for many strategic decisions, this bias is wrong. Even Amazon.com's Jeff Bezos and AOL Time Warner's Steve Case face some Level 1 or 2 uncertainty problems, such as whether to add new features to existing products, or which short-term alliances should be formed with software and hardware companies.

While companies in traditionally low-uncertainty environments could learn a lot from the Amazon.coms of the world, the reverse is also true: Amazon.com could probably learn a thing or two about strategic decision making from the BPs of the world. Decision makers in high- and low-velocity markets alike face strategy choices across all four levels of residual uncertainty, and thus they should be prepared to tailor their decision-making processes to reflect issue-specific uncertainty.

Finally, keep in mind that the level of residual uncertainty is also company-specific. If you do your homework better than others in the industry, have access to proprietary information, and avoid binary views of uncertainty, you may achieve 20/20 foresight and have a lower level of residual uncertainty than a competitor facing the same strategic issue. This foresight advantage may allow you to more proactively shape market uncertainty and craft strategies that are more likely to succeed in today's uncertain economy.

FROM UNCERTAINTY TO STRATEGY

The concept of residual uncertainty creates the right mind-set for decision makers in uncertain environments. It creates an expectation that systematic rigor is called for under uncertainty. It biases decision making toward the assumption that even seemingly high-uncertainty value drivers can and should be analyzed, and that such analysis often leads to strategic insight.

When a CEO asks his business unit manager, "What's the level of residual uncertainty around this proposed investment?" he creates an expectation that the manager will systematically determine what can be known and what cannot be known. If the CEO asks, "How much uncertainty surrounds this proposed investment?" he is more likely to get "High uncertainty" or "Not much" for an answer. Which response do you think the CEO would find more helpful in making his investment decision?

The concept of residual uncertainty, then, is the key to avoiding binary views of uncertainty. It helps lift the "uncertainty fog" surrounding many strategic decisions. That's reason enough alone to invest in an understanding of the level of residual uncertainty you face when making a decision. After all, the greater clarity you have on potential future outcomes—including those your own actions might help create—the better strategy choices you will make. That's certain.

But the concept of residual uncertainty does more than just create the right mind-set for strategic decision making. It guides you toward the right answers to fundamental strategy-under-uncertainty questions: Should you focus or diversify? Commit now or later? Attempt to shape or adapt to the uncertainty you face? It also guides you toward the right strategic-planning and decision-making processes: What new tools and frameworks belong in the toolkits of strategists facing uncertainty? How should strategists monitor and update their strategies over time in volatile business environments? If you know the level of residual uncertainty you face, you can craft better answers to these essential questions. The book's remaining chapters will show you how.

3

SHAPE OR ADAPT?

U SING THE FOUR LEVELS of uncertainty as your guide, you can achieve 20/20 foresight. And with this foresight, you'll be ready to make a crucial choice: whether to shape or adapt to the market. When you can foresee how the environment might change in the future, you can try to shape those changes to your advantage, or, alternately, prepare to adapt to them.

One might argue that any good strategy should attempt to shape *and* adapt, specifying actions designed to increase the probability of some outcomes while simultaneously preparing for other outcomes. That may work in some cases. But sometimes the actions a company must take to shape the market are inconsistent with those it would take to adapt to the market.

The QUALCOMM case mentioned in chapter 2 provides an example. For the last few years, QUALCOMM has been trying to shape the wireless telephone industry toward its CDMA technology. CDMA is a technical standard that determines how information travels and is communicated through a wireless network. CDMA is in competition with other technologies, including TDMA and GSM, to become *the* industry standard in the next generation of mobile phones.

If QUALCOMM wants to shape the industry, it realizes that it must build a coalition of support around the CDMA technology. This involves cutting deals with wireless companies to get them onboard, and convincing consumers that CDMA is superior. As QUALCOMM CEO Irwin Jacobs noted: "People have referred to it [the standards competition] as a religious war."[1]

To win this war, QUALCOMM must be totally committed to the cause (or at least look that way). If QUALCOMM tried to hedge its bet by producing chips for one of the competing technologies, too—something an adapter might do—it would undoubtedly undermine its shaping attempts. It would be hard for QUALCOMM to convince potential partners that CDMA was *the* superior standard if it was simultaneously making investments in competing standards.

As QUALCOMM illustrates, shaping actions are often at odds with adapting actions under uncertainty. As a result, shape *or* adapt is a real choice for most companies most of the time. Which one, then, should they choose?

SHAPING STRATEGIES AND ADAPTING STRATEGIES

Shaping Strategies

To make a sound choice, companies must fully understand their alternatives. There are five categories of shaping strategies. Each is designed to influence or even determine the outcomes of key, uncertain elements of industry structure and conduct.

CREATING AN INDUSTRY STANDARD

Some shaping strategies attempt to increase the probability that a preferred technology or business process becomes the industry standard. The QUALCOMM CDMA strategy is one example. JVC and Matsushita, in the way they shaped the VCR market toward the VHS standard (over Sony's Betamax alternative), is another. Microsoft and Intel, in the way they shaped the personal computer (PC) operating system toward their Wintel standard (and away from IBM's OS/2 and Apple's Macintosh), is a third.

The industry shapers in these cases designed their strategies to provide incentives for early adopters. The idea was that once a *critical mass* of consumers and producers adopted the standard, the standard would become increasingly valuable to other consumers and producers. This is the network externality effect described in chapter 2.

INTRODUCING PRODUCT, SERVICE, OR BUSINESS SYSTEM INNOVATIONS

A second set of strategies attempts to shape uncertainty by introducing fundamental product, service, or business system innovations into the market. These innovations might define new markets altogether or result in discontinuous changes in product costs or benefits in existing markets. When successful, these strategies shape markets because they redefine the basis of competition. DuPont in the introduction of nylon, Polaroid in instant photography, Netscape in Internet browsers, and Palm Computing in personal digital assistants all shaped markets through their product innovations.

Some well-known business system shapers include Wal-Mart, IKEA, Southwest Airlines, and Dell. Another is Calyx & Corolla, which shaped the flower-delivery business by pioneering direct-from-the-grower delivery that removed expensive middlemen and promised fresher, longer-lasting flowers.[2] Early e-commerce strategies also fundamentally re-shaped traditional retail business systems. Amazon.com in books is the most vivid example.

RESTRUCTURING THE INDUSTRY

Other shaping strategies focus on more basic industry restructuring. These strategies rely on traditional mergers and acquisitions, alliances, joint ventures, spin-offs, divestitures, and other actions that redefine the competition in uncertain markets. The goal of such strategies is to reconfigure the structure of the industry so as to strengthen the company's market position.

The Citicorp-Travelers merger, which formed Citigroup, was an example of using an acquisition in an attempt to shape the evolving, uncertain financial services industry. The parties involved believed that the Citigroup combination would be able to offer an unprecedented, full bundle of financial service products that would secure a leadership position in the industry.

Many other companies have attempted to shape through vertical integration, horizontal integration, or both. Intermountain Health Care, for example, shaped the evolving health care market in Utah, Wyoming, and Idaho by acquiring hospitals and physician practices and by launching a health insurance plan. Intermountain believed that its *integrated health care delivery system* would become the model for "medicine's next century" in the United States.[3]

Companies also attempt to shape evolving industry structure and conduct through horizontal and vertical *disintegration.* AT&T, for example, spun off its equipment provider, Lucent Technologies, in 1996. This allowed Lucent to reshape the telecommunications equipment industry: It was now free to sell to and partner and ally with other equipment and service companies without worrying about other AT&T businesses.

REPLICATING EXISTING BUSINESS SYSTEMS IN NEW MARKETS

A fourth set of shaping strategies focuses on replicating business systems in new markets. These strategies are not built around new products, services, standards, or business systems, but rather they focus on restructuring a market the company currently doesn't compete in. McDonald's, for example, implemented a highly successful strategy of shaping new geographic markets in the early 1990s by replicating its business system abroad. Similarly, Carrefour has replicated its business system and reshaped retail markets in a wide variety of emerging markets.

INFLUENCING COMPETITORS' CONDUCT

The last set of shaping strategies focuses on influencing the uncertain actions of competitors. DuPont, for example, shaped the uncertain capacity-expansion plans of its competitors in the titanium dioxide industry in the 1970s by building its own capacity ahead of market demand. I'll return to this example in chapter 4.

In another case, the Minnetonka Corporation (a diversified consumer goods company) successfully shaped its competitors' conduct in the liquid soap market. As sales of its innovative Softsoap product took off in the early 1980s, Minnetonka faced uncertainty over when and if major consumer goods companies like Procter & Gamble, Lever Brothers, and Colgate-Palmolive would choose to develop and market their own liquid soap brands. Minnetonka shaped these companies' entry decisions by committing to purchase the entire industry supply of the plastic pumps that were necessary to dispense liquid soaps. Without access to plastic pump supply, Minnetonka's potential competitors were temporarily prevented from entering the liquid soap market. Cornering the supply of pumps gave Minnetonka another eighteen to twenty-four months to build up its new liquid soap brand before facing strong competition.[4]

Shaping strategies, as the above examples illustrate, are designed to "get ahead" of uncertainty, driving industry change in a preferred direction. They may or may not end up being successful in shaping industry structure and conduct—witness Iridium's limited impact on the wireless telephone industry to date—but that is what they seek to do.

Adapting Strategies

Unlike shaping strategies, adapting strategies take existing and future industry structure and conduct as given. When the market is stable, adapters try to define defensible positions within the existing structure of the industry. When there is uncertainty, adapters attempt to win through speed and agility in recognizing and capturing new opportunities as the market changes. There are four categories of adapter strategies.

FOLLOWING A POTENTIAL SHAPER'S LEAD

The first category of adapting strategies involves quickly following a potential shaper's lead. Continental Lite, for example, was Continental Airlines' failed attempt to adapt its strategy to confront the uncertainty created by successful low-cost airline competitors. Compaq was a more successful adapter when it "bet" on industry shapers Microsoft and Intel with early alliances in the 1980s.

HEDGING AGAINST FUTURE POSSIBLE OUTCOMES

Other adapter strategies are designed to hedge against future market uncertainty. These work best when a limited, discrete set of paths that the market may follow can be discerned early. Software companies in the late 1980s, for example, could hedge against uncertainty over which PC operating system would emerge as the industry standard by developing products for each of the contenders (e.g., DOS, Windows, Macintosh, Unix, OS/2).

Likewise, Motorola's merger with General Instrument hedged uncertainty in broadband markets. If cable companies ultimately win the battle to wire homes with broadband access, General Instrument is the world's leading maker of cable converter boxes. This complements Motorola's strength in cable modems, where it already is the market leader. But if telephone DSL lines ultimately lead the broadband battle, the General Instrument deal gives Motorola a majority stake in Next Level Communications, a promising supplier of DSL technology. Either way, Motorola is well positioned to benefit from broadband growth.[5]

Probing through Continuous Experimentation

A third category of adapting strategies is built on constant experimentation in products, services, and business systems. The experimentation provides the company with the latest market information. This information helps the company tailor its strategy to the evolving industry structure, conduct, and performance. Capital One Financial Corporation uses such an experiment-based strategy to adapt to uncertainty in the credit card industry. In 1998, for example, Capital One conducted 27,000 tests of products, prices, features, packages, marketing channels, credit policies, account management, customer service, and collections and retention procedures.[6] Venture capital portfolios in high-velocity markets are also often built on this adapting logic. Each company in the portfolio represents a relatively small experiment that provides information the venture capitalists can use to adapt their portfolios to changing market conditions.

Building a Flexible Organization

A final class of adapting strategies is designed to build flexible organizations. Tactics often include staff development and retention programs, changes in governance processes, and investments in information systems that allow companies to adapt quickly to their changing environments. This is strategy as organization, not as market positioning. For example, many professional service firms spend little time thinking about the potential future evolution of their industries—or how they can shape or adapt to them over time. Nor do they offer their clients a continuous stream of new service line "experiments" to see what sticks. Instead, they focus on recruiting and developing professionals with general management skills, talented individuals that will allow them to identify and adapt to their clients' changing needs. Many early e-commerce entrepreneurs shared this philosophy, believing that raw talent would enable them to adapt their companies' strategies as the market evolved.

IS THERE A DOMINANT SOLUTION?

Given the many different examples of shaping and adapting strategies just described, it's obvious that business strategists don't believe there is a dominant one-size-fits-all answer to the shape-or-adapt question. In fact, even individual companies may not consistently choose one alternative over another across all issues, business lines, and time.

Whether a company chooses to shape or adapt depends on the strategic issue at hand—just as the level of residual uncertainty it faces is also issue-specific. For example, at the same time Capital One is using its experiment-based approach to adapt to uncertainty in U.S. credit card markets, it is fundamentally reshaping credit markets in the United Kingdom and Canada.[7]

Yet just because we observe companies following both shaping and adapting strategies doesn't mean that this is the right thing to do. Different best-selling business writers, in fact, argue that shaping, adapting, or a little bit of both is *the* dominant solution.

The organizational transformation agenda must be driven by a point of view about the industry transformation agenda: How do we want this industry to be shaped in five or ten years? What must we do to ensure that the industry evolves in a way that is maximally advantageous for us?[8]

Try a lot of stuff and keep what works.[9]

The dilemma of strategy in an uncertain, changing future involves balancing the need to commit to a future while retaining the strategic flexibility to adjust to the future.[10]

The first quote is obviously in the shaper's camp, while the authors of the second quote advocate experiment-based approaches that are common to adapters. And the third quote maintains that the best strategies lie right on the "edge" of shaping and adapting. Ultimately, which set of gurus is right—if any—is an empirical issue. Shaping or adapting is the dominant approach only if it leads to systematically better company performance across a wide range of strategic issues and market environments.

The data do not support a dominant, one-size-fits-all answer. McKinsey research suggests that while a substantial majority of the biggest business winners between 1985 and 1995 followed shaping strategies, adapters also thrived.[11] This research analyzed the fifty "stars" with the greatest sales, profit, and market capitalization growth during the sample period.[12] The stars included some of the computer and retail giants—Microsoft, Oracle, Sun Microsystems, Best Buy, The Home Depot, Wal-Mart—but they also included lesser known industrial (M. S. Carriers), business services (Omnicon), health care (Biomet), and financial services (Advanta) companies.

To be sure, these high-growth stars followed a variety of strategies over the ten-year sample period, depending on the situation. However, forty-three of the fifty stars (86 percent) followed predominantly shaping strategies. Most of the stars either fundamentally redefined existing business systems or helped shape an emerging industry's structure and conduct.

The small sample size and the analysis of only one ten-year time frame limit the general applicability of this study's results. In addition, since the study focused only on high-growth stars, one gets a skewed view of the benefits of shaping. Undoubtedly, many of the biggest losers in the sample period were shapers, too.

However, one of the study's findings is almost certainly robust: You don't have to be a shaper to win big. For example, Comair, the regional airline, became a high-growth star simply by following a standard adapter strategy.

THE IMPORTANCE OF UNCERTAINTY

With no easy dominant solution, how should strategists determine whether to shape or adapt? First and foremost, they must understand the nature and level of residual uncertainty they face.

Levels 3 and 4 uncertainty, for example, are often characterized by rapid, discontinuous change. Industry structure, conduct, and performance are all unstable. Technology standards are changing, competitors are constantly entering and exiting the market, and consumers have yet to lock in to a limited number of preferred brands.

Such markets offer the most headroom to implement successful shaping strategies. A series of major acquisitions, a bold technology investment, an aggressive product-bundling strategy—all may end up making order out of chaos. These are all high-stakes bets, but they have the potential to fundamentally reshape the market to a company's advantage.

With such opportunity before them, you would think that strategists would leap into the fray with newly minted shaper strategies. Yet the opposite occurs: Faced with unfamiliar uncertainty, they retreat into adapter strategies. Why? For incumbents, it's what they know best. Many have thrived in lower-uncertainty environments by securing positions in stable markets, and they relied on the traditional strategic-planning toolkit, which focuses on the fit between current company capabilities and the current market environment. In times of turmoil, it's understandable that these companies stick to what they know best.

This bias toward adapting strategies is less severe, but still prevalent, among new entrants, too. After all, many of their managers and financial backers have attended the same business schools as the managers and financial backers of the older companies. Strategies are thus often screened using the same planning and decision-making processes that bias incumbents toward adapt postures. As a result, strategies that could fundamentally reshape current and expected future market structures are dismissed, since they don't coincide with current collective wisdom.

Add in a dose of risk aversion—common to most incumbents and less swashbuckling new entrants—and you can see that companies are even more biased toward adapt postures at higher levels of uncertainty. It's ironic: Just as the potential to shape the market increases, the appetite (or courage?) to do so decreases.

The best way to confront this dilemma is to ensure that both shaping and adapting alternatives are carefully considered—regardless of the level of residual uncertainty. But if there is a bias in the process, it should lean toward *shaping* highly uncertain environments, not adapting to them.

Of course, shaping is not a feasible alternative for all companies in all situations. Shaping only makes sense if their actions *can* influence or even determine the future values of key, uncertain value drivers. For example, an industrial company faced an important regulatory uncertainty when considering a major foreign investment decision. No matter how much analysis the company did it could not come up with a precise forecast of the regulator's actions. Furthermore, analysis showed that the company had little or no influence over this foreign regulatory body. A shaping posture was not feasible in this case. The company had to develop a strategy designed to adapt to the regulator's unpredictable actions over time.

Similarly, Hewlett-Packard (HP) faced unpredictable ink-jet printer demand across different countries in the 1980s. At the time, HP was customizing its ink-jet printers for use in different foreign markets at the factory, and then shipping them in finished form to its warehouses. HP had decided that it was cheaper to customize the printers at the factory than in the field. The problem was that as demand in the various countries rose and fell unpredictably, HP often found itself with excess printers that were configured for one country and a shortage of printers configured for another.

This uncertainty created an ongoing supply-demand mismatch at HP's warehouses. But HP had little ability to influence total printer demand across the different countries. Therefore, it developed a strategy designed to adapt to this key uncertainty that was outside of its control. HP decided to postpone the customization of the printers until it had shipped them to the warehouses and had firm orders in hand. This would substantially decrease stock-out and inventory-carrying costs, while slightly increasing production costs (since customization at the warehouse was more costly). The net savings from this strategy were approximately $3 million a month, according to Corey A. Billington, who directed HP's strategic-planning and modeling group.[13]

On the other hand, when Netscape launched its Navigator strategy, Internet access and browser standards were still in flux and thus could be shaped. And when AT&T invested heavily in the cable industry, it had every right to believe it could accelerate the rate of customer adoption of broadband services via cable modems. Its actions in themselves might help fulfill this prophecy.

Shaping makes most sense, then, when uncertainty is high and can be influenced by a company's actions. This is a useful rule of thumb for decision making. But we can take this one step further. Levels 2, 3, and 4 are all "high" levels of uncertainty, but how one thinks about shaping versus adapting should vary considerably depending on which level a company actually faces. How does the shape-or-adapt choice vary across all four levels of residual uncertainty?

Level 1

In stable, Level 1 situations, strategists have traditionally tried to find the "best fit" between a company's capabilities and opportunities offered by the existing and expected future market. This is, by definition, an adapt posture. It is no surprise that adapting is the traditional Level 1 choice. In stable markets, shaping opportunities are often not readily apparent.

Level 1 adapter strategies have been traditionally designed to leverage and build on such structural advantages as economies of scale and brands. This view of strategy has its roots in industrial organization economics, and it was translated into useful practitioner frameworks by Michael Porter and others in the late 1970s through the 1980s.[14] In stable business environments, the logic goes, market and business system *positioning* choices erect entry barriers to competition and thus provide companies with unique opportunities to extract economic value.

Level 1 adapter strategies are also built around superior execution advantages. This is especially true in commodity markets—markets where companies have difficulty differentiating themselves on the basis of processes, products, brand, or even scale (the most common sources of structural advantage). As long as the company can stay a step ahead of the competition, superior execution can bring predictable returns in a stable environment.

This is not to say that Level 1 adapter strategies are free of risk. Companies that lock in to structural or execution advantages in stable Level 1 environments may still be susceptible to periodic bouts of industry upheaval—especially upheaval created by more aggressive shapers.

Even in relatively stable markets, creative business strategists regularly identify product, service, or business system innovations that better meet existing customer needs at more favorable costs. And if these innovations create enough potential value, they might displace firmly entrenched rivals.

For that reason, Level 1 shaping strategies are designed to create industry upheaval. Level 1 shapers seek to create discontinuities in stable, seemingly "mature" markets, purposefully raising the level of residual uncertainty for themselves and their competitors. They seek to create chaos out of order. As such, Level 1 shaping strategies are risky and uncommon. But there are examples. AutoNation's consolidation and national branding strategy was designed to fundamentally change the stagnant auto retail game. *USA Today* transformed newspaper markets to the extent that even the staid *New York Times* and *Washington Post* now feature color pictures. And Federal Express's original overnight-delivery strategy reshaped the sleepy mail-and-package-delivery industry.

Level 2

Whereas shapers in Level 1 seek to raise uncertainty, in Levels 2–4 they attempt to lower uncertainty—creating order out of chaos. In Level 2 environments, a MECE set of possible outcomes defines the future. Shaping strategies attempt to increase the probability—if not the certainty—that one of the outcomes most favorable to the company occurs. For example, JVC's VCR-licensing strategy was designed to shape the industry toward its VHS standard (rather than Sony's Betamax). And some Regional Bell Operating Companies (RBOCs) have attempted to shape regulations to allow them entry into long-distance markets, and manage the process by which new entrants can compete for local telephone customers. When a limited set of possible outcomes—in which one of them will occur—can be identified, shaping strategies focus on making the right one occur.

The hallmark of all successful Level 2 adapter strategies is the flexibility to compete and potentially thrive—regardless of which one of the distinct industry outcomes occurs. For instance, electric power generators, and others whose business depends on energy-intensive production processes, often face Level 2 uncertainty in determining the relative cost of different fuel sources. Distinct scenarios can often be identified; for example, either natural gas or oil will be the low-cost fuel. Many companies thus choose an adapter strategy when building new plants: They construct flexible manufacturing processes that can switch easily between different fuels.

Since Level 2 adapters must only prepare for a limited set of possible outcomes, such hedging strategies often make sense. PC software companies could hedge their strategies in the late 1980s, for instance, because there were only a limited number of operating system standards that could emerge into near-term market leaders.

Under Level 2 uncertainty, such hedging strategies are relatively easy to manage on an ongoing basis. A MECE set of possible outcomes usually implies that there is a distinct set of "signposts" that signal which scenarios are becoming more or less likely. Adapter strategies can be effectively managed over time by tracking these signals and updating the strategy based on the latest market and competitive intelligence. I will discuss this further in chapter 7 when I discuss contingent road maps.

Level 3

In Level 3 environments, a range of possible future outcomes can be identified, but a limited set of MECE outcomes cannot be. Shaping strategies in this situation focus on moving the industry toward the "right end of the range." They are not scenario-making strategies, but rather direction-setting strategies.

In the range of possible outcomes defining the market size and share of different wireless telephone technologies, for example, Iridium's shaping strategy was designed to increase the share going to satellite-based services. Internet banking strategies are designed to increase the share of financial service transactions taking place online. And a significant component of Monsanto's life-sciences strategy involves the acquisition of seed companies, in hopes that this will increase the rate at which farmers adopt Monsanto's genetically engineered seeds.

Hedging adapter strategies are not as desirable in Level 3 as they are in Level 2, since at Level 3 it is much more difficult than at Level 2 to determine if you've "covered all the bases." Instead, successful Level 3 adapters tend to focus more on *emergent* strategy development. As in Capital One's U.S. credit card strategy, they might use continuous experimentation to identify market opportunities as they evolve over time. Or like professional service firms, they may focus on building organizational capabilities ("strategy as organization") that will allow them to adapt and thrive no matter which direction the market turns.

In all Level 3 cases, successful adapter strategies are supplemented with an increased focus on monitoring market developments over time. Unlike Level 2 situations (where signposts, such as regulatory rulings, may be relatively clear), market signals at Level 3 are hard to spot (such as a relatively small market share shift). If a successful strategy is to emerge over time, companies must spot these signals as they appear—and react fast.

Level 4

When an entire industry is in flux, an industry shaper can bring the market to order. It can set an industry technology standard, consolidate a group of fragmented competitors, and even offer a new business model for the industry to emulate. The more uncertain the environment, in fact, the greater the chances that anyone willing to take a stand may be emulated by others.

This implies, paradoxically, that shaping strategies in Level 4 may deliver higher returns *and* lower risk than in situations with lower residual uncertainty. If you believe in a new industry standard, for example, and you are willing to invest in its development, this creates a "touchstone" for others to react to. You are, in fact, bringing some order to the market chaos. If you are a credible player in the industry, your commitment may well convince others to commit as well. Your belief in the new standard may set off a chain of events that creates a self-fulfilling prophecy. The credibility of Netscape's management team, for example, was a key factor in its successful attempt to set new standards for Internet browsers when it first launched Navigator.

The inability to anticipate or even bound the range of future market outcomes in Level 4 situations limits adapters' abilities to actively hedge their bets. Therefore, as in Level 3, adapters focus more on strategies that emerge as events warrant. Unlike Level 3, though, constant experimentation may not lift the fog of uncertainty. As a result, Level 4 adapters often focus on strategy as organization—making sure they have the right people, systems, culture, and governance processes in place to identify and adapt to opportunities as they become clarified over time.

Many of the top commercial and investment banks share these traits. They can't anticipate all future developments in emerging financial markets and resulting shifts in customer needs, so they focus instead on creating high-performing organizations that position their companies to successfully adapt as new opportunities emerge.

OTHER CONTRIBUTING FACTORS

While the nature and level of residual uncertainty help clarify the shape-or-adapt choice, they aren't the only important factors. Others include the company's external environment, internal capabilities, and aspirations.

External Environment

Shaping makes most sense when the market rewards innovators and first movers with sustainable, superior economic returns. Thus, shaping strategies are particularly relevant when network externality effects are present in a market. When these effects are present, shapers that can create a critical mass of consumers and producers around a new technology standard, business system, or product can build dominant market share positions that support monopoly profits (at least until the next successful shaper comes along). Industry-shaping attempts built around this logic include Netscape's Navigator and Iridium's satellite telephone standard.

Technology standards drive one form of first-mover advantage that shapers should look for in their markets. But there are many other forms of first-mover advantage that might justify shaping strategies. For example, first movers might build brand loyalty. They may lock up access to the best supply and distribution sources. They might build fundamental cost advantages based on experience. Or they might build privileged relationships with the most profitable customers.

To incur the higher risk often associated with shaping strategies, companies must ensure that a higher expected return through such first-mover advantages is likely. Not all industries and markets offer strong first-mover advantages (they may be ripe for shaping, but not offer shapers any significant returns for doing so). For example, it's not clear yet whether e-commerce pioneers like Amazon.com and eBay have established any meaningful first-mover advantages. By its very nature, the Web invites comparison shopping, which may undermine one of the most important potential first-movers advantages: brand and customer loyalty. Being an e-commerce adapter, then—replicating the good ideas and avoiding the bad—may offer similar returns to those won by pioneering shapers, without all the risk. Only time will tell.

The nature and range of possible near-term changes in a market also help strategists make shape-or-adapt choices. If change is expected to be continuous and incremental over time—providing a more limited range of possible outcomes within a given period—then adapting may be preferred. But if the environment is one of possible discontinuous change (foreboding a wide range of near-term outcomes), shaping may make more sense. Ultimately, the key issue is the *range* of potential outcomes—whether it is Level 1, 2, or 3 uncertainty (one cannot identify this range, by definition, in Level 4)—and whether or not it is possible to successfully adapt within that range.

Since adapters leverage their existing assets and capabilities to adjust their strategies as the market evolves, great market discontinuities—those that make obsolete these assets and capabilities—can make it very difficult to adapt successfully. In situations with greater potential for large discontinuities (and thus a wider range of potential outcomes), adapting may in fact be a high-risk strategy—perhaps even a higher-risk strategy than shaping.

Consider Kodak's digital photography strategy, for instance. It's not hard to imagine digital products some day wiping out traditional cameras and films. This is a projection that Kodak cannot afford to *adapt* to— because if it came to fruition it might be too late for Kodak to adapt its strategy without destroying the company. As a result, Kodak has been trying to shape the market transition to digital photography in a way that maximizes the probability of Kodak success. Given the magnitude of the digital challenge, Kodak really has no choice but to be a shaper.[15]

Adapting strategies are also most effective in markets with reasonably timely, reliable, and transparent information flows. In commercial- and investment-banking markets, for example, product and service innovations, demand drivers, and regulatory changes are fairly transparent to all competitors. The same can be said for many consumer retail and software markets. Adapters in such markets can quickly identify new trends and capitalize on them.

On the other hand, technology innovations and capacity-expansion plans can often be extremely opaque in commodity chemical markets. Since capacity and cost management are key value drivers in the industry, companies can suffer unexpected losses when they don't accurately perceive competitors' plans to add new capacity or technologies ahead of time. To avoid having to adapt to these unfavorable outcomes, chemical companies will often favor preemptive shaping capacity and technology investments themselves.

Summing up, besides the nature and level of residual uncertainty, the three most important external environment factors when making shape-or-adapt choices are: opportunities for first-mover advantages; the pace of possible change and thus range of possible future outcomes; and the availability of timely, reliable, and transparent information flows. Large, sustainable first-mover advantages and wider ranges of potential future outcomes favor shaping strategies. Information-rich environments favor adapting strategies.

Internal Capabilities

What a company brings to the table—or can soon acquire once at the table—is also essential to crafting winning shape-or-adapt choices. It is the fit between external market opportunities and company capabilities—relative to competitors—that defines the ability to create and capture value.

A company is usually better off if it can build its strategies around the valuable assets and capabilities it already owns. For example, it is almost unthinkable that Coca-Cola *wouldn't* design its strategies to protect and leverage the Coca-Cola brand.

Managers recognize the opportunity costs associated with not fully leveraging existing capabilities, and they often find it hard to consider strategies built around new capabilities. In most circumstances, this bias is fine. But there are situations when companies should actively consider, if not favor, strategies built around new sources of advantage that may render obsolete existing advantages.

In periods of rapid change, existing competitive advantages may lose value, and perhaps become competitive disadvantages. Technological or process breakthroughs, like the Internet, can destroy existing structural and execution advantages. Deregulation, globalization, and patent expirations can eliminate entry barriers that have been the traditional sources of advantage in industries like telecommunications, electric power, and pharmaceuticals. New business models, such as e-commerce, may decrease the value of existing distributor and customer relationships. In such situations, incumbents must be willing to revisit their fundamental assumptions about competitive advantage. A new business model may be required—even one that actively cannibalizes the core business and its competitive advantages, just as banks' financial service offerings on the Internet have cannibalized some of their bricks-and-mortar business.[16]

These new business models often require shaper strategies. In order to succeed, however, shapers must often change the incentives of other players to adopt new standards, reconfigure their business systems, create new demand, or enter or exit markets. To do so, shapers must be credible to other industry participants.

How do shapers demonstrate such credibility? Successful shapers share some common attributes:[17]

- *Clear visions for industry evolution.* Bill Gates (Microsoft) saw the utility of PCs in homes and offices; Fred Smith (Federal Express) of overnight package delivery; Dee Hock (Visa) of credit cards over cash; and Jeff Bezos (Amazon.com) of e-commerce. Visionaries of this caliber can take the market with them.

- *Deep pockets and an appetite for risk.* There is no doubt that shaping strategies backed up with the will and means to see them through are more credible. No one doubted Sony's commitment to minidisks, PlayStations, and Betamax, for example. Sony had the financial resources and the necessary tolerance for risk to ensure that its shaping attempts were credible to other players in the market.

- *Reputations and existing brands.* Did Netscape have extra deep pockets when it began shaping Internet browser standards? No, but it did have an extremely credible leadership team: Jim Clark had founded Silicon Graphics, which had gone on to revolutionize computer graphics. Marc Andreessen was a world-renowned "whiz kid" who had been a leading member of the team that developed Mosaic, the original browser that had turned the Internet from an academic's tool into a mass medium. And Jim Barksdale was the former head of AT&T Wireless Services, with unquestioned expertise as an enterprise software customer. When "Marc, Bark, and Clark" talked, their high-tech pals listened. Reputation—either embodied in a company's leaders or in its existing brands—can go a long way in certifying the credibility of shaping strategies.

- *Leadership position in a related business.* Of course, it helps if reputations and brands are built on true internal capabilities that are fundamental to successful shaping strategies. A leadership position in related markets or businesses is one signal of these capabilities. For example, Enron's leadership position in energy-trading markets demonstrates its market-making capabilities and makes its attempt to shape new bandwidth-trading markets more credible.

- *World-class technology and innovation skills.* Companies that consistently innovate—especially with discontinuous technology breakthroughs—are positioned to generate the ideas, products, and services that can shape markets. Hewlett-Packard, for example, has consistently reinvented printer markets over the last two decades based on its ability to innovate technologically. And Netscape's Navigator represented a discontinuous improvement over Mosaic and other early Internet browsers.

- *Operational excellence.* Credible shapers not only have strong structural positions and good ideas, but they also are known for world-class operational excellence. BP's Sir John Browne is highly regarded for his ability to command operational excellence, leading analysts to conclude that his high-stakes industry-shaping acquisitions will likely pay off.

- *Willingness (and ability) to share value.* Shapers must create "win-win" outcomes for other industry participants. When Visa developed standards for its credit card payment and processing, for instance, it ensured that card issuers and merchants stood to capture much of the value created in the system. This created the proper incentives for banks and other card issuers to issue and market cards, and for merchants to accept Visa.

- *Ability (and desire) to use alliances to fill in capability gaps.* Shapers call in friends to fill in where they are lacking. JVC teamed up with Matsushita in VCR development and commercialization in the mid-1970s. Without this partnership, JVC may not have had the deep pockets, structural position, or reputation to make its VHS standard a success.

This is a pretty formidable list of attributes found in successful shapers. As a result, managers often think of adapting as the easy or fall-back strategy alternative. This is a mistake on two fronts. First, it leads managers to assume that adapting doesn't require proactive strategic commitments like shaping does. Nothing could be further from the truth. Refer back to the section earlier in this chapter that lays out the categories of adapting strategies. Notice that "do nothing" is not one of the categories. In fact, following a potential shaper's lead, hedging against possible future outcomes, probing through continuous experimentation, and even building a flexible organization require real up-front capital commitments—financial and human—to succeed.

Second, it leads managers to assume that passive—not active—management is required to see the strategy through. In fact, adapting strategies often require more active management teams than shaping strategies do. While shaping strategies may front-load commitments in an attempt to capture first-mover advantages, successful adaptation is predicated on the ability to quickly *recognize* and *mobilize* to capture the opportunities the market offers as it evolves over time. Adapters must be adept at spotting opportunities and threats, and turning on a dime to reorient their companies when necessary.

Successful adaptation isn't easy. The material in chapter 7 can help your company do better. But before falling into an adapting strategy by default, conduct an honest assessment of your company's ability to actually adapt when called upon. And avoid at all costs the "do nothing" trap. Doing nothing is inconsistent with shaping and adapting. It's a third alternative altogether—one that I do not recommend.

Aspirations

Company aspirations—including long-term vision and mission, shorter-term performance goals, and risk tolerance—also play an important role in the shape-or-adapt choice. Suppose your company aspires to be number one or number two in every business it participates in (General Electric's old mantra). Chances are that your company will have to follow shaping strategies if it wants to achieve such lofty aspirations.[18]

There are other similarly straightforward links between company aspirations and shape-or-adapt choices, such as the risk-averse manager's preference for adapting. I have only two simple suggestions for making these links work better in practice. One, begin every strategy development process with an *explicit* discussion of the company's aspirations, including how these aspirations influence the strategy decision at hand, and any trade-offs the company is willing to make (for example, accepting a lower current profit rate in return for securing an advantaged position in a potential high-growth market). Two, revisit aspirations once *real* shaping and adapting alternatives have been identified and evaluated. Real alternatives help decision makers determine if their initial aspirations were unrealistically optimistic—or worse, overly pessimistic.

TO SHAPE OR ADAPT? MAKING THE RIGHT CHOICES UNDER UNCERTAINTY

As you make your own shape-or-adapt choices, the nature and level of residual uncertainty, the external market environment, and company capabilities and aspirations will all play an important role. Unfortunately, there is no explicit algorithm available for weighing each factor and making the right choice. Making these choices is often more of an art than a science. Nonetheless, the checklist of key questions in table 3-1 provides a good anchor for your deliberations. Use it to ensure that your company is considering all relevant factors when making its shape-or-adapt choices.

To illustrate how the checklist can help separate strategies that are likely to succeed from those that are likely to fail, we reconsider a few famous—and, in some cases, infamous—shaping choices through the lens of the checklist. Would the checklist have identified the likely winners and losers ahead of time?[19] Since the majority of business strategy problems face Level 2 and 3 uncertainty, we will consider two cases from each of these levels—one a success, one a failure.

Circuit City's Divx strategy provides an example of a Level 2 shaper that made the wrong choice. Divx competed with the standard DVD format for customers playing digital videodisks, a classic Level 2 situation where the key uncertainty was whether Divx or DVD would emerge as the industry standard.

Divx disks cost $4.50 for unlimited viewing during a forty-eight-hour period. After that, the customer could discard the disk or recharge the disk for $3.25 at any time for another forty-eight hours. Billing was automatic through phone lines that connected to the Divx player.

The Divx strategy was developed on the premise that customers would flock to the standard because it could play DVD formats as well, and because one could avoid the hassle of returning rentals to the video store. But Circuit City misread customers and other important players in

Table 3–1   Shape or Adapt? A Checklist of Questions

Uncertainty

☑ What level of uncertainty do you face? What would shaping and adapting entail given this level?
☑ Can you influence or determine the outcome of key uncertainties?

Other external-environment factors

☑ Are there significant first-mover advantages?
☑ Is change expected to be continuous and incremental over time, or discontinuous? What is the range of possible outcomes?
☑ Will you have access to timely, reliable, and transparent information flows?

Internal capabilities

☑ Are your company's current capabilities more in line with successful shaper or adapter attributes?
☑ Can you build the requisite capabilities to become a successful shaper or adapter?

Aspirations

☑ Are your company's aspirations more in line with shaper or adapter strategies?

the industry. First, customers were vehemently opposed to adopting a technology that could track what and when customers watched in the privacy of their own homes. Second, DVD disks often offered customer-preferred features like wide-screen formats that Divx did not. And third, retailers were reluctant to market Divx players because it meant handing royalties to Circuit City, which was a formidable consumer electronics competitor. By misreading the market, Circuit City's shaping Divx strategy was doomed from the start.[20]

Table 3-1 helps highlight the two main reasons why the Divx strategy failed. First, there were indeed first-mover advantages in establishing digital videodisk standards—and DVD had them! DVD had already developed a loyal base of customers, producers, and retailers that was reluctant to embrace a new standard. Divx did not offer enough incremental value relative to DVD to overcome this first-mover advantage—and in some aspects (like the availability of wide-screen formats), Divx was inferior to DVD. Second, Circuit City had a limited ability to influence others to adopt its standard. Retailers had to be willing to promote Divx for it to succeed. But they had no interest in propping up a strong competitor like Circuit City. As a result, Circuit City had limited leverage to increase the probability that Divx would win the standards war. A strategy that focused on increasing this leverage ahead of time—perhaps by creating a profit-sharing retailer consortium to align incentives behind Divx—might have been more effective.

Minnetonka, on the other hand, followed a successful Level 2 shaping strategy when it launched its Softsoap brand in the early 1980s. As explained earlier in this chapter, we know that Minnetonka faced Level 2 uncertainty over the market entry plans of its major potential competitors: When and if would Procter & Gamble, Lever Brothers, and Colgate-Palmolive follow Minnetonka's lead and enter the liquid soap market? Minnetonka took decisive action that helped to shape this key uncertainty, which enabled it to build a vital new business that it then sold to Colgate-Palmolive for $61 million in 1987.[21]

Minnetonka employed several tactics that were responsible for the success of its shaping strategy. The checklist helps one to understand these tactics. Minnetonka built three first-mover advantages relative to the consumer goods giants.

First, by being the first to enter the market, Minnetonka built up a market-foresight advantage over its potential rivals. Minnetonka began test-marketing Softsoap in 1977, and by 1980 the product had proved itself to be viable by consistently capturing between five and nine percent of the test-market share of total bar-soap sales. By 1980, these market tests gave Minnetonka the proprietary information it needed to conclude that there was Level 1 uncertainty around the size of the liquid soap market. This information enabled Minnetonka to embark on a national advertising and product launch campaign while its potential competitors were still unsure of the extent of liquid soap demand, and as such were still considering only limited market tests.

Second, as an aggressive first mover, Minnetonka was able to lock up key suppliers of essential liquid soap dispensing parts and thereby prevent competitors from quickly scaling up their own businesses. In the early 1980s, there were only two suppliers of the plastic pumps that dispensed liquid soap. Minnetonka locked up both suppliers' total capacity by ordering 100 million pumps to support its national rollout strategy for Softsoap. This tactic not only influenced the competitors' conduct—Minnetonka's source of Level 2 uncertainty—but dictated it in the short-run. The plastic pump shortage prevented competitors from making a full-scale entry into the market for eighteen to twenty-four months.

Third, Minnetonka did not have to worry about the potential cannibalization of existing soap brands when it launched Softsoap, while potential competitors like Procter & Gamble did. Procter & Gamble would naturally take a wait-and-see approach to the liquid soap market, because it would rightfully assume that most liquid soap sales—if they ever materialized—would come at the expense of bar soap brands like Ivory. In addition, Procter & Gamble and the other consumer goods majors would not risk degrading their existing brand names by applying them to an unproven new market. These brand advantages in the bar soap market actually created initial disadvantages in the liquid soap market, as the majors couldn't move aggressively without putting their existing franchises at risk. Minnetonka turned these incumbent disadvantages into its own set of attacker advantages, and as a result, successfully shaped its Level 2 uncertainty over competitive conduct and built a profitable business.

Iridium's attempt to shape the emerging satellite telephone industry is our Level 3 failure example. Iridium faced uncertainty over the total market demand for mobile telephone services and the price and performance attributes of satellite telephones versus other mobile alternatives (the driver of relative market shares). Iridium's $5 billion investment in a satellite network was designed to grow both the entire market and satellite's share at a faster rate.

Iridium had the right aspirations to be a shaper. But it fundamentally misread the market environment. To quote the *Washington Post* on the day after Iridium filed for chapter 11 bankruptcy protection:

> *Iridium's tale is one of a company that spent years getting a product to the market, and then found the market very different than it expected. The company was conceived at a time when conventional cell phones were expensive and rare. When it finally switched on its service last fall, cell phones were cheap and plentiful the world over and few people wanted costly, heavy Iridium phones.*[22]

Iridium's miscalculation may have been even more fundamental than that. The $5 billion that Iridium put into its satellite network represents an enormous fixed cost base, suggesting significant economies of scale. The key to success in such businesses is often to generate volume that lowers average unit costs and improves profitability, even if relatively low prices are necessary to achieve incremental volume. But according to some market analysts, Iridium's satellites were designed to handle no more than 1,100 simultaneous calls each. In other words, the business model required economies of scale to pay off, but the business system didn't support such scale.[23]

Iridium also ran into internal capability constraints that worked against its shaping play. New chief executive John Richardson admitted that Iridium "singularly failed" in its "commercial skills," noting that "our marketing was inept . . . and the products didn't work" at the time of the company's very public service launch (remember those ubiquitous ads in airline magazines?).[24] And finally, Iridium mishandled stakeholder communications, consistently surprising the market with performance well below expectations. The bad press generated by these surprises poisoned potential customers, investors, business partners, and employees' view of the likelihood of Iridium success.

Returning to table 3-1's checklist, a major driver of Iridium's failure was the inability to influence one key uncertainty: the rate of price and performance improvements in nonsatellite mobile telephone alternatives. Iridium was betting that it could get to market faster with a better alternative. It didn't, and thus it missed out on any significant first-mover advantages. Also, while Iridium had the requisite technical skills, it didn't have the marketing and commercial skills to pull off a market-shaping entry strategy. These two failures sealed Iridium's fate.[25]

Enron provides an example of a successful Level 3 shaping strategy. In the mid-1980s, Enron was a gas pipeline business with large levels of debt in an industry that was being rocked by deregulation. Enron, however, realized that vertical disintegration and market-based pricing in deregulated markets would open up a valuable business opportunity for intermediaries to manage new price and volume risks. The demand for this service was hard to predict, and Enron's shaping strategy focused on creating a market with substantial trading volume.

Enron launched its Enron Gas Services intermediary business, and it quickly added a number of risk management tools to its portfolio, including swaps, options, futures, and other unique contract provisions. By the early 1990s, Enron had created and dominated this gas intermediary business, and it was well positioned to extend its model to deregulating electric power markets around the world. As noted in chapter 2, it has even recently extended the model to create a market for bandwidth capacity.

Why did Enron's shaping strategy work? Go back to the checklist. First, it was grounded in the external environment: There was in fact a unique business opportunity to manage price and volume risk in deregulating markets, which Enron's customers valued. Enron's insight about the natural gas market was based in sound microeconomic logic. Second, Enron took steps to build the required capabilities. Certainly, as a regulated natural gas pipeline player, Enron did not have the existing skills in-house to make the commodity risk intermediation business a success. So, Enron poached risk managers from Wall Street and the best business schools, reworked compensation packages, and created an entrepreneurial culture within which its intermediary business could thrive. At the same time, Enron also leveraged its existing pipeline assets to manage required gas flows.

Third, Enron set aggressive aspirations that provided incentives for managers to quickly build intermediary skills and grow the business. Enron had the aspiration "to become the first natural gas major," and it set quantitative targets, such as 40 percent of earnings at any time coming from new businesses and annual earnings per share growth of at least

15 percent. Enron had true foresight about the market potential, created aspirations that motivated managers to capture this potential (and get to market first), and was successful in building the necessary risk interme-diation skills.

Like Enron, your company, too, can craft winning strategies that either shape or adapt to the residual uncertainty it faces. The level and nature of residual uncertainty help define feasible alternatives, while other aspects of the external environment, company capabilities, and company aspirations further inform your choice. In any case, 20/20 fore-sight that identifies what you can make happen—or what can happen to you—is a prerequisite for making the best shape-or-adapt choices.

4

NOW OR LATER?

R EGARDLESS OF whether you choose to shape or adapt, in order to succeed you must make the right commitments at the right time. Which markets should you enter and exit, and when? Which R&D programs should be funded, and which should be abandoned? Where and when should you build new plants? These are the questions that determine your company's future, and they keep you awake at night.

Your insomnia is understandable. Major commitments are difficult to make. Think about the decision to marry. Marriage is *uncertain* (no one can be certain the partnership will last) and partially *irreversible* (most couples won't get out of it without emotional and financial damage once the commitments are made).

To deal with this uncertainty and irreversibility, most people try to buy information and time. We call it dating. Through dating, they hope to resolve the uncertainty surrounding the potential match. Dating has a downside, however: Drag it on too long, and a potential mate may preemptively end the relationship. We call it getting dumped. That's the risk.

Uncertainty and *irreversibility* make it difficult to decide whom to marry. Uncertainty and the risk of *preemption* make it difficult to decide when to marry.

Similarly, uncertainty, irreversibility, and the risk of competitive preemption also affect the decisions of business strategists. Like the divorcée, a company that places the wrong bet may have to write off its sunk costs and redirect its strategy. Circuit City, for example, incurred a $114 million charge against earnings and eliminated 300 jobs when its Divx strategy failed.[1]

Meanwhile, a company that seeks always to "keep its options open" (like the perpetual bachelor) by postponing full-scale commitments may have its market opportunities shut down by more aggressive competitors. In *The Innovator's Dilemma: When New Technologies Cause Great Firms to Fail,* for instance, author Clayton Christensen chronicles how Sears, Roebuck and Co., Digital Equipment Corporation, and other former market leaders were displaced because they waited too long to respond to disruptive changes in their industries.[2]

Like worried mothers fretting over their unmarried sons, traditional strategy frameworks have long pressured corporate decision makers toward full-commitment strategies. These frameworks were developed in the days when business environments were more stable and thus predictable (or at least when we were willing to assume that they were more stable and predictable). In those times, delaying a decision would provide very little new information, but it would heighten the risk of competitive preemption. Thus, for companies facing Level 1 uncertainty, deciding when to commit—now or later—has always been simple: Commit now.

At higher levels of residual uncertainty, however, deciding when and how much to commit to a strategy may not be so straightforward. If there is no threat of competitive preemption, though, the answer is still easy: Postpone the commitments or stage them over time, until better information about the future is available.

But what should you do when there is both high uncertainty *and* a high probability of competitive preemption? This is the relevant question for today's most pressing strategy issues. Whether you are a cable company making a broadband investment decision, a pharmaceutical company formulating a gene therapy strategy, or a financial services provider building an e-commerce business, you face the same challenge: You must commit to a speculative strategy in a highly uncertain environment in which there are first-mover advantages (and thus significant risks of competitive preemption). If your strategy fails, the company is out of a lot of money, and you may be out of a job. This is no easy decision.

BIG BETS VERSUS REAL OPTIONS

How should companies decide when and how much to commit under such circumstances? Even companies facing Levels 2–4 uncertainty can take some actions that will deliver positive payoffs no matter what the future brings. Companies should commit to these *no-regrets* moves immediately. No delay, no regrets.

Implementing these no-regrets moves helps companies avoid the decision paralysis that can be so common in periods of rapid change. In the early 1990s, for example, U.S. electric power utilities faced great uncertainty over the form and pace of deregulation. But they knew for a fact that generation markets would become more competitive, and that local retail markets would eventually be opened to competition. Based on that knowledge, regional monopolists like PECO Energy, now part of Exelon Corporation, moved forward with power plant cost reductions and investments in building wholesale and retail sales and marketing skills. These were no-regrets moves—regardless of how deregulation played out.

Strategy under uncertainty, however, isn't merely a no-regrets game. Strategists under Levels 2–4 uncertainty invariably face choices that carry some risk. If key uncertainties play out favorably, these investments will deliver positive returns. But in other cases, they will incur losses.

Faced with such risky choices, strategists can respond in one of two general ways. First, they can make immediate, full-scale commitments— like the bachelor proposing marriage after the first date. These *big bets* often resemble high-stakes lotteries, involving irreversible commitments that will deliver large positive payoffs in some future scenarios, but large losses in others. Iridium's $5 billion satellite network investment is one example. If demand for Iridium's satellite telephone service were large enough, this big bet would pay off big. Low demand, however, would result in substantial losses. And in the low-demand scenario, Iridium could not expect to recover much of the cost it had sunk into its network by selling its assets to another satellite company.

A second approach is to postpone, stage, or make more flexible commitments in an attempt to manage risk—like the bachelor continuing to date for a longer period of time. Iridium, for example, could have funded a series of limited service trials with global business travelers and other potential customers before making a full-scale commitment to the $5 billion network.[3]

By postponing, staging, or making more flexible investments, strategists minimize irreversible commitments. As a result, downside losses in even the worst-case scenarios are limited. At the same time, if these actions also build privileged positions—say through better information, lower costs, stronger partnerships, or other competitive advantages—to make full-commitment decisions later, they may maintain access to the highest payoffs. Strategists that choose this approach are trying to create a more *asymmetric* payoff structure—small downside but large upside—across the range of possible future outcomes.

Financial options have such asymmetric payoff structures. Call options, for example, give holders the right—but not the obligation—to buy an asset (such as a share of stock) over a predetermined period at a fixed exercise price. If you purchase a call option on a stock, the most you can lose is the price paid for the option. However, if the price of the stock rises above the option's exercise price, then you gain all of this upside. In other words, the downside is capped, but the upside isn't.

Real options are investments in real capital, relationships, capabilities, and other tangible or intangible assets that offer the asymmetric payoff profiles associated with financial options. Deciding when and how much to commit under uncertainty boils down to making a choice between taking a big bet action (and making a full-scale commitment today) or investing in a real option to postpone, stage, or make more flexible commitments. In order to determine whether big bet or real option actions are more likely to create and capture value, companies should first define a feasible set of big bet and real option alternatives.

REAL REAL OPTIONS

Big bets—now-or-never, all-or-nothing choices—are relatively easy to recognize and evaluate. But real options are harder to get a handle on. It isn't always clear whether there are ways to postpone, stage, or make more flexible commitments without being shut out of substantial upside gains. How can you tell whether you have *real* real option alternatives to now-or-never big bets?[4]

Real options give companies the flexibility and preferential positions required to reoptimize their strategies as the business environment evolves. They make it easier to build on existing commitments (reinvest), change strategic direction (divest), or launch altogether new strategies (invest). In doing so, they create the characteristic asymmetric payoff profile of financial options, which have less downside than upside. To recognize a real option, then, look for actions with asymmetric payoff profiles, ones that build flexibility and preferential opportunities to reinvest, divest, or invest in the future. In particular, look for three types of real options: *growth, insurance,* and *learning.*

Growth Options

Growth options provide a preferential position to *reinvest* in the future, thus creating opportunities to capture the upside potential that may accompany uncertainty. This privileged position might be the result of economies of scale, scope, or other forms of market power (such as brand strength, proprietary access to supply and distribution channels, licenses or patents, or privileged relationships). Or it might be the result of superior information about consumers and competitors. In any event, this preferential position provides the right, but not the obligation, to scale up current operations, move into the next generation of products in your current market, or move into related products or markets.

For example, growth options include alliances, acquisitions of small players, and other limited-commitment market entry strategies. These allow companies to build skills, lower costs, and learn more about the profitability of a market before deciding to exercise this growth option and ramp up their investment.

Other growth options facilitate moves into the next generation of technology or products in the market. Intel's early-generation microprocessor businesses, for example, built brand recognition, customer relationships, and superior performance positions that Intel continues to leverage today in its products.

Growth options can also facilitate moves into related products and markets. Enron's Gas Services business, for example, built risk intermediation skills, commodity trading skills, and customer relationships that it has leveraged to create a large portfolio of products and services to manage volume and price risks in: power, crude oil, pulp and paper, steel and bandwidth markets.

Insurance Options

Insurance options provide a preferential position to *divest* in the future. This may involve either scaling or closing down operations, or switching to another strategy altogether. Insurance options protect against the downside losses associated with uncertainty by facilitating quick and relatively inexpensive changes in strategic direction.

Investments that limit business exit costs are good examples of insurance options. Outsourcing arrangements, flexible work and union rules, and shorter-term supply and distributor contracts are all investments that might facilitate exiting a business.

Along with limiting business exit costs, some insurance options also make it easier to scale back operations. For example, airlines often buy options to cancel or change orders when purchasing airplanes from Boeing or Airbus.

Insurance options can also facilitate switching to a different strategy. These switching options often build flexibility into the business system itself, providing operating flexibility. For example, electric utilities invest in generators that can be fueled by either oil or natural gas, depending on fuel prices. In addition, insurance options can also provide fundamental strategic flexibility. For example, a corporate law firm that hires the "best" general problem solvers, while building alliances with specialists, can more easily switch tracks as demand evolves across different industries and legal issues (such as antitrust, tax, or international trade).

Learning Options

Learning options provide a preferential position to *invest* in the future. They allow a company to postpone commitments until more information is available, or until the company has the requisite skills to make these commitments. Learning options protect against the downside losses often associated with premature big bets under uncertainty.

Early new product trials are learning options. These provide key information—plus some marketing and production skills—that give

companies a preferential position from which to make full-scale investment decisions later. Time itself, in fact, can be an important learning
option. An oil company holding a lease giving it the right to begin oil
exploration and production (a growth option), for instance, might wait
until oil price forecast uncertainties are clarified before deciding whether
to exercise its growth option.

Growth, insurance, and learning options are not necessarily mutually
exclusive. Any given action may provide all three sources of option
value. For example, a limited joint venture as part of a new market entry
strategy is a growth option. Why? Because it provides preferential access
to distribution networks and customers, and it may build useful brand
recognition should the company decide to ramp up its market presence
later. The joint venture can also be negotiated with a favorable, relatively
hassle-free exit clause, providing the company with a valuable insurance
option. Finally, the joint venture is also a learning option, since it postpones major investment decisions in local plants and distribution networks while providing privileged information on the market, its customers, and its competitors.[5]

Real growth, insurance, and learning options generate asymmetric
payoff profiles. These occur when an investment achieves the following:

- *Creates competitive advantage.* To maintain the upside potential of
  full-commitment actions, real real options must create preferential
  positions relative to competitors that don't own equivalent options.

- *Maintains flexibility.* Real real options must provide the right, *but not
  the obligation,* to exercise the option to reinvest, invest, or divest in
  the future. They must give managers the flexibility to reoptimize
  without locking them in to any one course of action.

- *Is highly leveraged.* The cost of making a full-commitment investment should be a high multiple of the cost of creating or buying a real
  real option. If not, the investment is more like a big bet that doesn't
  protect against the potential downside losses associated with large
  sunk cost investments.[6]

Using these three criteria, it is easy to see that not all partial-
commitment actions are real real options. Some don't build competitive
advantage, and thus don't maintain access to the high payoffs that full-
commitment strategies open up. For example, a newspaper is considering launching an online news service. It is unwilling to make a full

commitment to the strategy at this point, however, and it decides instead to just create a Web site. Is this a real growth option? It certainly is highly leveraged: The cost to create a Web site is a small fraction of the cost to develop a complete online news service. And it does leverage managerial flexibility because the Web site in no way obliges the newspaper to complete development of the online news service.

However, this investment in no way creates an advantaged position to launch the news service later. The Web site provides no differentiated information on customer needs and doesn't build content creation or technology capabilities. In sum, the Web site might be a good idea in its own right—but it certainly is not creating a valuable growth option for the future launch of an online news service.

Other actions do not maintain managerial flexibility. When wireless telephone companies purchased radio spectrum licenses auctioned off by the U.S. government, for example, they were making major future investment commitments: License owners were prohibited from reselling their licenses until they had built out wireless networks to minimum specifications. These licenses gave owners both the right *and* the obligation to use the spectrum for wireless services.[7] Most oil exploration and production licenses, on the other hand, give companies the exclusive right—but not the obligation—to develop a block of land over a fixed period. These licenses do not commit their owners to make further, significant investments, and thus they are real real options.

Still other actions are not leveraged enough to be considered real options. Consider this: A businessman wants to open a nightclub on Miami's South Beach. If he purchases the property, is this a real growth option? The property provides a privileged position, but not an obligation to start the business. However, property acquisition costs in South Beach make up a high percentage of the total costs involved in launching the business. Since the option is not highly leveraged, the businessman is actually making a bet—and not purchasing a real option—when he acquires the property.[8]

Real real options, on the other hand, meet all three criteria. Consider the first phase of a pharmaceutical R&D program, for instance: It creates privileged information—and perhaps patents—that provide an advantaged position from which the company can decide to reinvest or divest. It is also highly leveraged. The initial research phase usually accounts for only a small percentage of drug development costs, and it does not lock the company into full-scale development. Phase 1 research provides the right, but not the obligation, to continue drug development and commercialization.

Dating is another genuine real option. It provides information on potential match quality, and it preempts potential competitors (Jane can't go out with Joe Saturday night if she's already out with Jack). It is highly leveraged, as a date incurs much lower sunk costs than a marriage does. And it provides the right, but not the obligation, to go on further dates or to commit to marriage. Dating has the asymmetric payoff structure that many singles look for when faced with irreversible marriage choices under uncertainty.

MAKING THE RIGHT CHOICE: SOME GENERAL PRINCIPLES

Suppose you're about to make a big bet investment and you identify a real real option alternative instead. Which should you choose? In most cases, real options do not promise all the upside payoffs associated with big bets. It is usually costly to postpone or stage commitments—especially when one accounts for the opportunity costs associated with losing out on market opportunities to more aggressive competitors. Most strategists thus face the following trade-off when choosing between big bet and real option alternatives: Real options better manage downside risk, but big bets open up the greatest opportunities for upside gains. Understanding and managing this trade-off is the key to making the right choice.[9]

This trade-off also drives the shape-or-adapt choice. For example, chapter 3 argued that winning shaper strategies are often built around big bets designed to capture first-mover advantages. On the other hand, winning adapter strategies—especially under high uncertainty—often focus on real option plays that maintain the flexibility to tweak or revise strategic direction later on. But there is no one-to-one correspondence between the shape-or-adapt and big-bet-or-real-option choices. Most shapers *can* postpone and stage commitments to at least some degree without substantially decreasing their probability of success. When and how much to commit has been a fundamental choice for Amazon.com, for example, as it has attempted to shape e-commerce markets. Likewise, all adapters must ultimately pull the trigger on some big bet commitments. It's impossible to keep all options open indefinitely.

For shapers and adapters alike, it all comes down to when and how hard to pull that trigger. The right choice depends on which alternative promises to create and capture the most economic value for the company.

In uncertain situations, where reliable point forecasts of cash flows are not obtainable, how should companies value big bet and real option alternatives to make the right choice? For years, decision makers have struggled with this valuation issue, often relying on gut instinct when traditional discounted cash flow valuation tools failed to properly account for uncertainty. Recent advances in real option valuation (ROV) techniques, however, allow companies to implement more quantitative, fact-based decision-making processes.

Some of these quantitative ROV techniques are developed later in this chapter. However, it is not always necessary to use these quantitative tools. Sometimes, a set of qualitative decision-making rules—based on the analogy between real and financial options—can help you decide whether a big bet or real option is the best play. Let's develop these qualitative rules first before moving on to the quantitative tools.

Suppose you were making a choice between buying 100 shares of Microsoft today, buying a call option to purchase these shares later at a fixed exercise price, or avoiding Microsoft stock altogether. Buying 100 shares is a full-scale commitment today, while buying the option is a more flexible partial-commitment approach. Which one is more valuable?

The relative value of options versus outright stock purchases is determined by four key parameters:[10]

1. *Stock price uncertainty.* If you buy the stock today, you are exposed to both upside and downside fluctuations in the stock price. If you buy the option, on the other hand, your downside loss is limited (you won't exercise the call option if the stock price falls below the exercise price) but you still maintain rights to the upside gains. Thus, higher uncertainty favors options over outright stock purchases.

2. *Duration of the option.* The more time you have to exercise the option, the more likely it is going to be "in the money" at some point. Longer option duration favors options over outright stock purchases.

3. *Dividend payments.* Owners of stock receive dividend payments; owners of options do not. The greater the expected dividend payment, the more you forgo by owning the option on the stock instead of the stock itself. Higher dividends, then, favor outright stock purchases over options.

4. *Risk-free interest rate.* This is the appropriate discount rate for evaluating the option. The greater the discount rate, the greater the opportunity cost associated with making a full-scale stock purchase today (instead of postponing that decision until the future). Thus, higher risk-free interest rates favor options over outright stock purchases.

Buying a call option on Microsoft stock, then, will be preferred to an outright stock purchase when: the uncertainty over Microsoft's stock price is high, the duration of the option is long, dividend payments to Microsoft shareholders are low, and the risk-free interest rate is high.

Using the analogy between financial and real options, then, it follows that real options are favored over big bets when:

- *There is high uncertainty over the expected cash flows from full-commitment investments.* By providing the flexibility to reoptimize over time, without incurring significant up-front sunk costs, real options leave open opportunities to capture the upside of uncertainty, while limiting the downside. When there is little or no uncertainty, big bets are preferred (in fact, these commitments are more like no-regrets moves in this case).

- *The real option has a long duration without threat of competitive preemption.* The longer one can realistically postpone or stage a commitment—longer real option duration—the more valuable a real option is relative to a big bet. This duration is largely determined by the level of competitive intensity and thus risk of competitive preemption (when you don't have proprietary rights to an investment). Other times the duration is determined by contracts (a company has the contracted right to buy out another's stake in a joint venture during a specified period) or other legal institutions (a patent gives a company the right to commercialize intellectual property over a specified number of years). In general, the more proprietary an investment opportunity is, the slower the pace of change in the business environment, and the lower the competitive intensity, the more likely that a real option will have longer duration (and thus, all else equal, be more valuable than big bet alternatives).

• *The real option incurs limited direct and opportunity costs to maintain.* Dividend payments lower the value of call options because they represent foregone cash flows that are only available when you commit to owning the stock. Similarly, real options—that are either very expensive to maintain or are subject to competitive preemption— forgo large cash flows relative to big bet alternatives. For example, staged R&D programs or limited market entry joint ventures often require significant ongoing expenditures to keep options for future reinvestment viable. The more expensive these ongoing "option maintenance" expenditures are, the more likely that big bets should be preferred. The competitive preemption issue is also paramount here. Environments with strong first-mover advantages and other drivers of aggressive competitive preemption favor big bets over real options.

• *The risk-free discount rate is high.* The more a company discounts the future, the more valuable it is to the company to postpone and stage commitments over time. For example, consumer durable goods and housing purchases decrease in times of high interest rates. Even if you don't have to borrow to finance your big bets, the opportunity cost of this capital is higher, favoring real options over big bets.

These four rules can point strategists in the right direction when determining how to time and scale commitments under uncertainty. Understanding the trade-off between uncertainty and competition is essential to making the right choices: High uncertainty favors real options, and greater competition favors big bets.

The four rules help explain why I'm married, while my good friend Jack is still a bachelor. Jack prefers dating over marriage because he's convinced that he's still young enough to meet new people (long real option duration), he hasn't met anyone yet that he is sure is right for him (high uncertainty), he prefers cheap dates (low cost to maintain the option), he has never had a girlfriend initiate a breakup with him (low perceived risk of competitive preemption), and he "lives for the moment" (high discount rate).

On the other hand, I'm married because I'm certain my wife and I were meant to be together (low uncertainty) and I have always been someone who looks to the future (low discount rate). In any event, I am confident that both Jack and I have made the right decisions. The four rules clarify why my full-commitment decision makes sense, and why Jack is better off keeping his options open.

The four rules might also explain why, for a given business opportunity, one company might prefer a preemptive big bet investment while another company prefers to stage commitments over time. For example, consider the recent investment decisions Airbus and Boeing have made in the market for superjumbo-jets. Airbus has made a $10.7 billion commitment to bring its new 600-seat A380 model to market. Boeing, on the other hand, has decided not to develop an entirely new plane for the superjumbo-jet market at this time. Instead, Boeing has planned a $4 billion upgrade to the 747, creating a 747X model that it expects to directly compete with the A380.[11]

Why has Airbus arguably chosen to "bet the company" on the A380, while Boeing has followed a more staged, partial-commitment approach? An examination of market analyst and business press interpretations of the strategies pursued by both sides suggests that they may be consistent with the four rules. For example, consider the following quotes from articles published in *The Economist* and *Business Week:*

1. "Airbus, of course, has had some special help: soft loans, worth one-third of the development cost, from the German, French and British governments. These are to be repaid with interest through a levy on sales, but the governments share some of the commercial risk, so Airbus is getting capital more cheaply than it might on the open market."[12] *The Economist* appears to be arguing that access to low-cost capital is one reason why Airbus has made its preemptive, big bet commitment to the superjumbo-jet market. This is consistent with the rule that *lower risk-free discount rates favor big bets over real options.*

2. "With more streamlined systems," says Credit Suisse First Boston analyst Pierre Chao, "Boeing could even churn out its own superjumbo in the future if customers demand it, faster and for less money than Airbus was able to."[13] This market analyst appears to be arguing that one reason Boeing has made a smaller commitment

to the superjumbo-jet market at this point is that the company believes it can launch a superjumbo-jet of its own later if the market proves to be profitable, without loss of significant first-mover advantages to Airbus. Using the terminology introduced above, Boeing's partial-commitment real option strategy has a long duration. Boeing's strategy is thus consistent with the rule that *real options with long durations are favored over big bets.*

3. "Boeing believes that the entire market for such gigantic planes could number fewer than 350, of which it expects to grab 50% with enhanced 747s. . . . Airbus contends the potential is much larger, some 1,500 units. . . . By choosing to invest $4 billion to extend the 747 rather than churning out a whole new plane, Boeing is banking on the lower estimate."[14] *Business Week* appears to be arguing that Boeing has both a lower-mean and higher-variance estimate of superjumbo-jet market size than does Airbus. The Boeing and Airbus strategies are thus consistent with the rule that *higher uncertainty favors real options over big bets.*

4. "Boeing's stock is riding high because its factories are humming smoothly at full capacity, and its order-book is strong. . . . Many at the company, not to mention its shareholders, feel that this is no time to bet the firm on a risky investment as big as the A3XX."[15] *The Economist* appears to be arguing that, as the market leader in today's jumbo-jet market, Boeing is not forgoing significant current sales by not offering a superjumbo-jet alternative. As the second player in the jumbo-jet market, however, Airbus has less to lose and more to gain than Boeing does by launching a superjumbo-jet to compete directly with existing jumbo-jet models. Using the terminology introduced above, if Airbus were to delay its commitment to the superjumbo-jet market, it would experience higher opportunity costs than would Boeing. The Boeing and Airbus strategies are thus consistent with the rule that *real options are favored over big bets when they incur limited direct and opportunity costs to maintain.*

While it is unclear whether the market analyst and business press interpretations presented above are grounded in hard facts—whether Airbus has a significant cost of capital advantage, for instance, is the subject of ongoing debate—it is clear that if these interpretations are correct then both Airbus and Boeing are taking the right approach to the superjumbo-jet market. All four rules suggest that Airbus is the natural player to make a preemptive big bet in the superjumbo-jet market, while Boeing should keep its options open.

KnowledgeCube Group (KCube), an early-stage venture capital firm headquartered in New York City, provides another example.[16] KCube makes small investments (typically $.5–5 million in return for 10–50 percent of the start-up's equity) in "Stage 0" (just an idea and a leadership team) high technology companies and accelerates their growth by providing strategy and technology consulting, investment banking, and other professional services through its network of partner organizations. KCube seeks to grow these companies so that they are well positioned for the next round of venture financing or strategic investment. At this point, KCube coinvests on preferential terms or cashes out.

Each KCube investment is thus a partial-commitment real option play. Why is this KCube's preferred approach (as opposed to taking larger, big bet stakes in its portfolio companies)?

1. By maintaining formal and informal relationships with "bleeding edge" technology centers such as the Massachusetts Institute of Technology Media Lab and Stanford Computer Science Lab, KCube identifies companies for investment that have just begun to develop new prototypes. The commercial viability of these technologies is often not yet clear, so KCube companies face high uncertainty over their future cash flows.

2. KCube has a shorter investment horizon than most private equity investors. KCube believes that its partner network adds most value during the first six to eighteen months that a company exists. After this initial period, KCube believes that traditional private equity investors like Kleiner Perkins Caufield & Byers or strategic buyers like Sun Microsystems are more natural owners. This is why KCube seeks to either coinvest with one of these players or cash out. During this short time frame, and given the extreme uncertainty in its market spaces, there is little threat of competitive preemption. In other words, there is little chance that a competitor company will emerge and establish itself as the industry standard, thereby closing off future financing for KCube's companies. A real option play is less risky and thus more favorable under these circumstances.

3. KCube chooses companies that are likely to have low cash "burn rates," thus minimizing the costs of keeping these real options in play. By aggregating purchasing power and seeking synergies across its portfolio businesses, the company can also maintain a relatively low burn rate over time. In addition, KCube executives and partners take on key management roles in their portfolio companies, formulating strategies, recruiting board members and managers, and developing customers. All of these actions limit the opportunity costs associated with foregoing a big bet financial commitment to KCube's portfolio companies.

4. KCube built its initial capital base to invest in portfolio companies in 1999 when the expected annual return from technology company investments was over 50 percent. The opportunity cost of KCube's financial capital was thus quite high, suggesting a high discount rate, favoring real option plays over big bet alternatives.

Finally, consider DuPont's titanium dioxide strategy in the 1970s.[17] In 1972, there were seven U.S. manufacturers of titanium dioxide (a whitener used in paints, paper, and plastics). DuPont was the market share leader at 34 percent. Raw material shortages and new environmental legislation suddenly gave DuPont's proprietary process technology a 15 percent unit cost advantage over National Lead (the second-lowest-cost player) and a 25 percent unit cost advantage over high-cost players.

DuPont considered two alternate strategies to leverage this cost advantage. Its *grow* strategy would involve adding new low-cost capacity to capture all expected growth in the industry through 1985, resulting in an expected market share of 65 percent. The *maintain* strategy, on the other hand, would keep market share relatively stable over time by limiting DuPont capacity expansion. This strategy would focus on maintaining conduct and margins in the market, while the grow strategy was willing to sacrifice short-term margins for long-term market share leadership.

It appears that DuPont considered competitive conduct uncertainty *the* primary issue in deciding between the grow and maintain strategies. A limited set of discrete scenarios was identified, based on the capacity decisions of different competitors. Therefore, DuPont saw this as a Level 2 strategy issue, with competitive conduct being the primary source of uncertainty. Public records show that DuPont was concerned that if it did not increase share, then "competitive expansion and the resulting scramble for sales will affect price."[18]

In addition, if competitors built capacity, "DuPont would then no longer be an industry leader and would be facing the prospect of competing on a 'me too' basis," the public records reveal.[19] In other words, DuPont worried that if it followed a maintain strategy, competitors would implement their own grow strategies and weaken DuPont's competitive position. So, if DuPont could preemptively implement its own grow strategy, it might drive competitor incentives toward maintain or shrink strategies.

Given DuPont's focus on competitive conduct uncertainty, it made sense for DuPont to implement the grow strategy. In 1973, DuPont announced it was studying the feasibility of a new plant in De Lisle, Mississippi, and it publicly committed to the project in 1974. In the meantime, it foiled attempts by several competitors to lead industry prices upward, in a bid to keep prices low relative to unit reinvestment costs. The first line at De Lisle started up in 1979. When combined with incremental capacity additions at existing plants, DuPont achieved a 57 percent market share by 1981. None of DuPont's competitors added capacity during this time. The preemption strategy had worked as planned.

But, in retrospect, would a real option play, one that added capacity incrementally, have worked better? DuPont was correct in assuming that its preemptive capacity additions would drive competitors away from adding their own new capacity. But while focused on competitor conduct uncertainty, DuPont may have overestimated demand for titanium dioxide.

Indeed, the titanium dioxide industry suffered a severe and unexpected downturn during the 1970s, largely as a result of the general macroeconomic malaise brought on by stagflation. This eventually led DuPont to delay and even cancel some previously announced capacity additions, and it had a significant impact on the profitability of its new capacity.

If DuPont had perceived this demand uncertainty ahead of time, it is likely that it would have been more cautious in staging capacity commitments over time. The "real options lens" would have been more important in its decision-making process, highlighting the benefits of deferment and flexibility. As it was, DuPont addressed the problem primarily through the "competition lens," and this steered it toward the grow strategy.

As the DuPont case illustrates, sometimes one of the four rules suggests a big bet, while another suggests a real option. In such cases, these qualitative rules can only take you so far in making better strategy choices. You may be able to intuit your way to the right answer. But ROV techniques—which help *quantify* the trade-offs between higher uncertainty and greater threats of competitive preemption—can help you test this intuition.

NOW OR LATER? LEVEL 3 (AND EVEN LEVEL 4) ROV TECHNIQUES

To understand how ROV works in Level 3 situations, consider an oil company that wants to value a five-year license for exploration and production on a particular block of land.[20] Suppose there is Level 3 uncertainty around the profitability of the block, driven by underlying uncertainty over the block's oil reserves and future oil prices. This uncertainty allows one to bound the range of future revenues from the block, but the range is so wide that the choice of whether to acquire and develop the block is not obvious.

These oil licenses pass our criteria for real options: They provide the purchaser with a privileged position (only the license owner can explore or produce on that block of land), they are highly leveraged (licenses cost little relative to full exploration and production costs), and they provide flexibility (companies have the right, but not the obligation, to explore and produce on the block). Buying a license and postponing block development may be more valuable than an immediate full-scale commitment to exploration and production, if time will help resolve uncertainty over the price of oil and the block's reserves.

The Black-Scholes option-pricing model was designed to value *financial* options under Level 3 uncertainty.[21] It defines six drivers of option value, four of which I highlighted in the previous section. These six drivers also determine real option value under Level 3 uncertainty. The six drivers as applied to the oil example are the following:

1. *Stock price.* This is the current price of the stock for which the option is bought. According to finance theory, this price should reflect the present value of all expected future cash flows associated with owning the stock. The higher the stock price, all else being equal, the higher the value of a call option to purchase the

stock at a given exercise price. The equivalent measure in real option valuation is the present value of cash flows expected from the investment opportunity on which the option is purchased. For example, if the block is expected to yield 50 million barrels of oil to be sold at a cash margin of $10/barrel (in present value terms), the "stock price" in this case is $500 million. The value of the license obviously rises as these expected cash flows rise.

2. *Exercise price.* This is the predetermined price at which the option can be exercised. The higher the exercise price, all else equal, the lower the value of a call option to purchase the stock at this price. The real option equivalent is the present value of all sunk costs that will be necessary to capture the cash flows expected from the investment opportunity. In valuing oil block licenses, this is the present value of the costs necessary to develop the field for production, assumed to be $600 million in this case. The value of the license falls as these costs rise.

3. *Uncertainty.* This is captured by the standard deviation of the per-period growth rate of expected future cash flows from owning the stock. While the stock price reflects the expected value of these cash flows, this standard deviation measure reflects the degree of uncertainty around this expected value. As noted previously, higher uncertainty increases option value. For real options, uncertainty is measured by the standard deviation of the per-period growth rate of cash flows from the investment opportunity. There are two main sources of uncertainty around cash flows from the oil block: the quantity of oil it will produce and the cash margin on that oil. In this case, these uncertainties implied a 30 percent standard deviation on the annual growth rate of cash flows. The license would be worth even more, however, with a 40 percent standard deviation. Since the company would never choose to exercise the option to develop the field unless cash flows were expected to cover the $600 million development costs, the greater downside is irrelevant. The greater upside, however, implies that there is a higher probability of earning large profits.

4. *Option duration.* This is the time remaining during which the option can be exercised. Option duration increases option value because it provides more time for the option to be "in the money."

For real options, the analog is the period for which the investment opportunity is available. In general, this will be determined by technology (length of a product life cycle), intensity of competition, and contract length, including patents, leases, and licenses. In this case, the option duration is five years, since the license provides proprietary access to the block for that time. The license would be worth more if it had a longer duration.

5. *Dividends.* Dividend payments lower option values since they drain cash from the company during the duration of the option. The real option equivalent is the cash that is lost during the duration of the real option. This includes costs that are necessary to keep the opportunity alive, and cash that is forfeited to competitors that make preemptive investments. In the license case, one doesn't have to worry about competitive preemption on the block (the license is proprietary). However, a company does have to pay $15 million per year—or 3 percent of the expected value of future cash flows—to keep the reserve active and available for possible development. The license would be worth more if these annual upkeep expenses were lower.

6. *Risk-free interest rate.* In both real and financial options, this is the yield of a risk-less security with the same maturity as the duration of the option. A higher risk-free interest rate increases option value. With a high risk-free interest rate, there is a high opportunity cost associated with making full-scale commitments today relative to postponing or staging these commitments over time. In the oil block license case, the risk-free rate is 5 percent.

Given these parameters, what should the oil company do? Proceed with full-scale development of the block today? Purchase a license to the block and delay development? Or do nothing? The payoff to doing nothing is obviously zero. The expected payoff to immediate full-scale development is also easy to calculate. It is the present value of expected cash flows minus development costs minus the cost to acquire a license to the block. This is $500 million minus $600 million minus the cost of the license.

Unless someone pays the company $100 million or more to develop the block (a negative license price!), the company is better off doing nothing than embarking on full-scale development today. But should the company still acquire the license, even though it doesn't pay to begin immediate development? Using the Black-Scholes option-pricing formula, we find that the license is worth $100 million.[22] As long as the company can obtain the license for $100 million or less, its best alternative is to buy the license.

Why is the license worth $100 million when the expected value of developing the block today is *negative* $100 million? What accounts for this $200 million difference? The difference is the ability to reoptimize later. If tests indicate the block will yield more than 50 million barrels, or if oil prices rise, the company can decide (with better information) to develop the block. Even though the block is "out of the money" today, there is a good chance that it will be "in the money" in the future, and the license gives the company a proprietary right to this money. The value of this future right to develop, then, given the parameters of the oil block in this example, is $100 million.

A company that approaches the block with a real options mind-set instead of an all-or-nothing, now-or-never one will value the block more highly. By recognizing the flexibility to defer development over the lifetime of the license, and the ability to learn more about the profitability of the block over time, the company with a real options mind-set can acquire licenses that others would ignore. While a license to the block in our example is worth $100 million, if other bidders take an all-or-nothing, now-or-never mind-set to the deal—and since the block is currently out of the money—a company may be able to acquire the license for next to nothing!

This is not just a hypothetical case. Anadarko Petroleum of Houston used real options analysis in bidding for a block of oil rights in the Gulf of Mexico, where the potential was vast but highly uncertain. The option paid off: In 1998, Anadarko announced that it had made a major oil and gas discovery there. Michael D. Cochran, Anadarko's vice president for worldwide exploration, explained that the company was willing to pay more for the rights because it realized the real options available in the license. "Most people looked at it and just saw the minimum case," he said. But Anadarko recognized the upside and valued it properly.[23]

As the Anadarko case illustrates, the key to using the Black-Scholes model to value real options versus big bets under Level 3 uncertainty lies in identifying the right parameters for the six value drivers. Of course, this is easier said than done. But it can be done, and the oil license case provides some hints on how to do it. Let's take it one parameter at a time.

- *Stock price.* History and geology are the best guides here. By studying blocks with similar geological characteristics that have already been explored and produced, the oil company can generate an expected oil production figure. Likewise, by consulting expert forecasts of future oil prices—as well as forward market prices—it can settle on an expected price path. Together, these forecasts determine the expected cash flows from full exploration and production of the block.

- *Exercise price.* Experience is also the best guide here. By analyzing the costs to fully explore and produce similar blocks, the oil company can generate an estimate of the cost to exercise its option to develop this block.

These first two parameters are the standard inputs into NPV analysis. What's the expected NPV of a full-commitment strategy to develop the block right away? Expected future cash flows from the investment (stock price) minus up-front costs of the investment (exercise price). Since most companies attempt to complete some sort of NPV valuation of their strategies, estimates of these first two ROV parameters are often already on hand (even if they are difficult to obtain).

It often requires incremental information and analysis, however, to generate estimates for the four remaining ROV parameters.

1. *Uncertainty.* If history is the best guide for expected oil production from a given block, it can also tell you the standard deviation of such production. Likewise, historical oil price variance (and variance in expert forecasts) allows you to estimate the standard deviation around annual oil price forecasts. Together, these provide an estimate of the standard deviation around the growth rate of future cash flows from the block. In fact, the ability to make this estimate is what defines this license acquisition problem as a Level 3 issue. If such an estimate were impossible to obtain, this would be a Level 4 issue instead.

2. *Duration.* In this case, it is easy: The license provides proprietary rights to develop the block for five years. When real options aren't proprietary—and thus subject to competitive preemption—com-

petitive intelligence will be necessary to determine how long the option will likely remain viable before being closed off by a more aggressive competitor.

3. *Dividends.* History again provides the necessary information. The oil company can study previous oil exploration and production projects to determine the annual expenses that were necessary to keep similar blocks viable for future development.

4. *Risk-free interest rate.* This parameter is easy. All the company has to do is find a U.S. government security (or similar "risk-free" corporate bond) with the same duration as the option to peg this discount rate.

History and forward-looking expert forecasts define ROV parameters in the oil license case—and many other cases with Level 3 uncertainty. But what's a strategist to do when there is no history, no expert opinion, and no quantitative data to estimate ROV? In particular, what if he faces Level 4 uncertainty and can't estimate the essential uncertainty parameter? Are ROV techniques inappropriate in this case?

Even in these circumstances, ROV techniques allow the strategist to work backward to determine "what you would have to believe" to support a given strategy. For example, suppose the oil company could purchase the above oil block license for $50 million, but it didn't know what uncertainty parameter to use in valuing the license. The Black-Scholes formula allows it to back out the following solution: As long as the standard deviation of the growth rate of cash flows is greater than 17 percent per year, the license is worth it. Similar sensitivity analyses allow strategists to determine what they would have to believe about other ROV parameters to support real option strategies over big bets (or doing nothing). Clarifying what you would have to believe about such parameters does not provide a straightforward strategy prescription (as would be possible under lower levels of uncertainty), but it does provide a useful benchmark for decision makers facing Level 4 uncertainty.

Rigorous Level 3 ROV analysis can also be applied to many drug development cases. Consider Biogen's decision to commercially develop Avonex in the early 1990s.[24] Biogen owned the patent on Avonex, a drug that had just been approved by the U.S. Food and Drug Administration to slow the progression of disability in relapsing forms of multiple sclerosis. Biogen faced Level 3 uncertainty over market demand for the drug, and thus it was considering whether to launch immediate commercial development of the drug (a big bet) or delay its launch until more precise demand forecasts were available (a real option).

The solution lay in the six drivers of real option value.

1. *Stock price.* This was the expected present value of operating cash flows associated with selling Avonex in the market. Market research was used to size the market and estimate the price Biogen could charge. This research estimated that the expected value of bringing the drug to market, absent initial development costs, was $3.422 billion.

2. *Exercise price.* This was the initial cost of developing the drug for commercial use. History and forward-looking expert analysis provided the estimate: $2.875 billion in this case.

3. *Uncertainty.* There was no objective, project-specific estimate of uncertainty available for the Avonex launch. The average annual standard deviation of firm value for publicly traded biotechnology stocks, however, was considered a good proxy measure for this uncertainty—47 percent in this case.

4. *Option duration.* The option's duration was assumed to be the Avonex patent life, or seventeen years. During this period, Biogen had the proprietary right to bring Avonex to market. Upon patent expiration, it was assumed that market competition would erase any excess returns Biogen could earn on Avonex.

5. *Dividends.* Every year that Biogen delayed commercialization of Avonex, it would lose a year of patent-protected cash flows. To delay one year, then, costs one-seventeenth, or 5.89 percent, of the $3.422 billion in total expected cash flows. As time goes on, this loss represents a higher percentage of total possible cash flows from the drug (the "dividend rate" would rise to one-sixteenth, or 6.25 percent, after a one-year delay, one-fifteenth, or 6.67 percent, after a two-year delay, and so on). This implies that even if it paid to delay commercialization in the first year, eventually it would make sense for Biogen to bring Avonex to market.

6. *Risk-free interest rate.* The current long-term Treasury bond rate was the right benchmark, 6.7 percent.

Given these parameters, what was the right answer for Biogen? The NPV of immediate commercial development was a healthy $547 million ($3.422 billion minus $2.875 billion). At the same time, the Black-Scholes formula showed that the value of the patent itself—including the option to defer development to future years—was $907 million. The implication? Biogen should defer commercial development of Avonex for at least one year even though the NPV of an immediate development strategy was positive.

The intuition is clear.[25] High uncertainty over future cash flows coupled with a reasonably low cost of delay (only forfeiting one-seventeenth of total potential cash flows, with no threat of competitive preemption) implies that it is worthwhile to delay development. The delay may allow for better information on the commercial prospects of the drug, and result in better decisions to develop the drug—or not—later.

Biogen could also use the Black-Scholes formula to back out what it would have to believe to reverse its choice, and begin developing the drug immediately. For example, the formula showed that if the standard deviation of the cash flow growth rate were below 20 percent (instead of the 47 percent assumed above), immediate development would be preferred. With lower uncertainty, the opportunity cost of delay would outweigh the gain. Similarly, if the dividend rate were above 8.3 percent (instead of the assumed 5.89 percent), Biogen would opt for immediate development. This higher rate implies higher forfeited earnings associated with delaying investment.

The oil license and drug patent cases illustrate that financial option-pricing models like Black-Scholes can be adapted to provide prescriptive insights on the scale and timing of real commitments under Level 3—and even Level 4 if you are willing to work backward—uncertainty.[26]

NOW OR LATER? LEVEL 2 ROV TECHNIQUES

The Black-Scholes model assumes continuous Level 3 uncertainty, and thus it is not directly applicable to real option versus big bet choices driven by Level 2 uncertainty. When faced with Level 2 uncertainty, however, simple decision-tree approaches can provide close approximations—if not exact calculations—of the value of big bet and real option strategy alternatives.

Consider the following disguised case, based on observations taken from several different international retail markets. Acme (a fictitious name) was a diversified retailer with a leading position in its home geographic market. Globalco (also a fictitious name) was a highly innovative retailer that had developed a new store format in a different geographic market. This format was a hit with consumers in Globalco's home market, and as a result Globalco was stealing significant market share from retailers with traditional store formats such as Acme's. As Globalco's position strengthened in its home market, however, market analysts believed that it would soon be seeking to enter international markets in order to sustain its rapid growth. This situation created a major Level 2 uncertainty for Acme: Would Globalco choose to invade Acme's home market with its new store format?

Given this uncertainty, Acme had three strategy options: (1) maintain its status quo strategy, (2) commit to and launch a new full-scale chain of retail stores modeled after Globalco's store formats (a big bet) in its home market, or (3) build a few pilot stores modeled after Globalco's store formats with the option to launch a full-scale chain later if Globalco did indeed enter the market (a partial-commitment real option). These potential actions are summarized in the decision tree shown in figure 4-1.

If Acme decided to maintain its status quo strategy, it would avoid cannibalizing its existing stores. However, this strategy would probably encourage Globalco to enter Acme's home market within the next five years. Analysts, in fact, put that probability at 90 percent if Acme maintained its status quo strategy. Since NPV analysis showed that Acme would lose \$500 million (discounted back to the present) if Globalco invaded, the expected value of this strategy was $(0.9*{-}500) + (0.1*0) = -\$450$ million.

On the other hand, if Acme built its own new full-scale chain, it could potentially preempt Globalco's entry. To be sure, it would cannibalize its own stores, and the strategy would require an initial \$200 million capital investment. However, analysts believed that the possible preemption effect of this move would be quite strong: If Acme followed this path, analysts placed the probability of a Globalco invasion at only 20 percent. Rerunning the NPV analysis for this scenario, it was estimated that if Globalco did enter, Acme would lose \$275 million; if Globalco did not enter, Acme would only lose \$125 million. The expected value of this strategy was thus $-200 + (0.2*{-}275) + (0.8*{-}125) = -\$355$ million.

Figure 4-1 Acme's Pilot Store Strategy

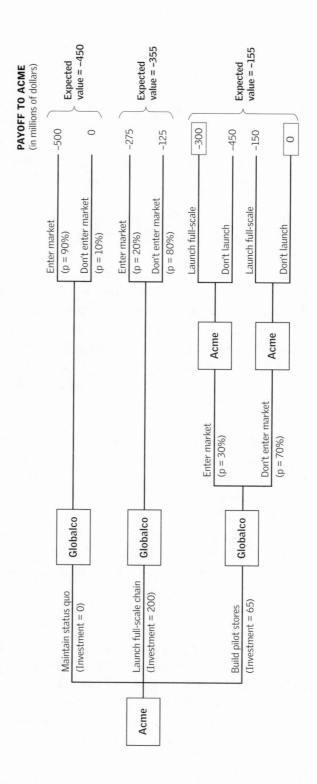

But there was also a middle ground. Instead of a full-scale new store format rollout, Acme could launch a limited number of pilot stores for an initial $65 million investment. This strategy might serve to preempt Globalco's entry into the market, and would position Acme in any case to compete more effectively if Globalco did enter the market. In addition, the pilot stores wouldn't cannibalize much of Acme's existing business. The analysts were consulted again, and they concluded that if Acme followed this path, the probability of Globalco entering Acme's market was 30 percent.

To value Acme's pilot store strategy, where choices are staged over time, you must start at the end point of the decision tree and work backward. For example, if Acme found itself on the "limb" in which Globalco staged a full invasion, it would be in Acme's interest to respond with a full-scale chain of its own. It would lose $300 million in this case, but such a response would still be Acme's best option under those trying circumstances. On the other hand, if Acme found itself on the limb where Globalco had not entered the market, it would be in Acme's interest *not* to launch a new full-scale chain. Acme's earnings would not change in this case. Calculating the expected value of the option strategy, making sure to take into account the fact that Acme would respond optimally to Globalco's future entry decision, we see that the expected value of the pilot store strategy was $-65 + (0.3*-300) + (0.7*0) = -\$155$ million.

The partial-commitment pilot store strategy was obviously the best choice for Acme. While the strategy still had a negative expected value, its value was much higher than the other two alternatives. The pilot store program made it less likely that Globalco would enter the market, and it avoided (or at least postponed) major capital investments and significant cannibalization of Acme's existing stores.

The Acme case also illustrates a key difference between NPV and ROV approaches. NPV mechanically discounts back expected cash flows, while ROV starts at the end of the decision tree and works back one decision at a time, always asking "What would an intelligent manager choose to do at this point given the flexibility to reoptimize?" When managers do have the option to reoptimize, and when they will in fact exercise that option, then ROV provides a more accurate valuation of any investment or other strategic decision.

NPV is appropriate for valuations of Level 2 strategies that have limited or no flexibility. However, any strategy built on managerial flexibility to reoptimize as Level 2 uncertainty unfolds should be valued with ROV decision-tree techniques. Otherwise, strategies with flexibility will be *systematically undervalued relative to full-commitment strategies, biasing decision makers away from real options and toward big bets.* Choosing the right valuation technique is not then just a matter of familiarity or convenience; it has real strategic implications for the types of strategies your company will choose to employ.[27]

NOW OR LATER?
QUALITATIVE RULES AND QUANTITATIVE TOOLS

Companies that thrive under uncertainty avoid decision paralysis and make the right commitments at the right times. It's easy to move forward with no-regrets moves. But for riskier strategies, the timing and scale of commitments often determine business winners and business losers. You will make better commitment decisions—choosing the right set of real options and big bets—if you adopt the qualitative rules and quantitative tools developed in this chapter and tailor them to the level of residual uncertainty you face. Developing 20/20 foresight can't turn all of your strategy choices into no-regrets moves. But it can point you toward the right set of rules and tools for deciding when and how much to commit in an uncertain world.

5

FOCUS OR DIVERSIFY?

WE ALL KNOW that when faced with high uncertainty, it is rarely wise to put all of our financial investment eggs in one basket. It's hard to find a financial advisor today that doesn't view diversification as a sound, long-term investment strategy. But we also know that a well-placed bet on the right stock will always outperform a diversified portfolio. That's why, whenever our financial advisors think they have a comparative advantage in valuing a stock (say through privileged access to an equity analyst who has proven to understand an industry sector better than his peers), they urge us to move cash out of our mutual funds and place a bet on their undervalued star.

Business strategists must also decide whether to focus or diversify their investments. A focused strategy—investing in one unproven technology at the expense of another, for example—may in some cases deliver extraordinary returns, but in others, it may deliver nothing but massive losses. A more diversified *strategy portfolio* (making smaller investments in each technology, for instance) may promise more stable returns, but, of course, it forfeits the potential upside gains of a well-placed bet. In crafting winning strategies under uncertainty, managing this potential risk-return trade-off is essential.

Under what circumstances should companies choose diversified strategies, and when should they choose more focused strategies? The financial investment analogy provides some clues. How we respond to a financial advisor's hot tip often comes down to two factors: our tolerance for risk, and our trust in the advisor's apparent comparative advantage in valuing the stock. In such cases, I've asked myself, "Does my advisor really have a special source of foresight about this stock's future value?" Because if she doesn't—and the stock's potential is common knowledge—then the current share price already reflects my advisor's positive future outlook. More often than not, I tell her, "thanks, but no thanks." Admittedly, I'm a risk-averse investor. But it is this foresight-advantage question that usually convinces me to keep my money in the mutual funds.

Similarly, a risk-averse management team is more likely to build a diversified strategy portfolio. So are managers who have a binary view of uncertainty, those who treat all uncertainties as unknowable (they certainly have no foresight advantages).

The financial investment analogy, though, goes only so far in helping business strategists make better choices. While you should be skeptical of financial advisors who claim they can systematically beat the market through foresight advantages, business strategists who embrace the concept of residual uncertainty and achieve 20/20 foresight *can* systematically outperform their more myopic competitors. They do this by placing focused strategy bets—while competitors are still waiting for the fog of uncertainty to lift.

There's another important difference. The average financial investor cannot influence stock market prices. When deciding whether to focus or diversify his portfolio, the uncertainty he faces about future stock prices is outside his control.[1] Yet business strategists, as noted in chapter 3, often *can* shape their uncertainties. A focused strategy is a pretty safe bet if it shapes the market in a way that virtually ensures success.

Foresight advantages and shaping opportunities are two reasons why a manager might choose a focused strategy for his company. But, like the shape-or-adapt and now-or-later choices I discussed in the previous two chapters, there are no easy, one-size-fits-all answers. This chapter lays out the factors you should consider when choosing between focused and diversified strategies.

FOCUS OR DIVERSIFY? FRAMING THE QUESTION

There are many reasons why a company might want to diversify its strategy portfolio. At the corporate level, complementary business units might achieve economies of scope through shared corporate services, assets, and cross-selling opportunities. Stable, profit-generating businesses might fund the start-up costs for new businesses. The corporation might be able to develop better, deeper management talent by exposing its young stars to a diverse set of business issues.

Much has been written about these drivers of diversification decisions. And since this book is on strategy under uncertainty, I won't go into them. Rather, this chapter focuses on when diversification is the best way to manage risk under the various levels of uncertainty.

By focusing on risk management alone, this chapter takes a fairly narrow look at the focus-or-diversify question. Yet when defining what is meant by diversification, this chapter takes a broad approach. Any strategy that seeks to manage risk by one of three methods—*classic diversification, hedging,* or *insurance*—will be considered a diversified strategy. The question, then, is whether a company should use one or more of these three methods when faced with issue-specific uncertainty, or whether it should instead make a focused bet.

Classic Diversification

All three risk management methods have analogs in the financial markets. Classic diversification, which is like buying a broad-based mutual fund, manages risk by making a collection of independent strategic investments that have uncorrelated payoff structures and risks. If some ventures fail, others will probably succeed—and the performance of the overall portfolio will be acceptable.

When crafting real, as opposed to financial, strategies, classic diversification works best if each investment has a real options payoff structure, so that investments that fail incur only small losses, but investments that succeed maintain high upside payoffs. Diversification through a series of big bets is less desirable. It is impossible for all but the largest companies to diversify through big bets. These, after all, may each require many millions if not billions of dollars of up-front investment costs. Even a series of small bets is usually not a good diversification strategy: Returns for such bets tend to be symmetric—small upside and downside—so that the overall diversified strategy portfolio would usually earn a limited return. Diversification through real options, on the other hand, leaves open the opportunity for high returns, while protecting against downside losses.

To manage uncertainty around the changing tastes of consumers and the evolving risks in credit card markets, Capital One, as I mentioned earlier, maintains a broad portfolio of independent product and service experiments. Each experiment is low cost, but each may be ramped up into a broad new product or service line if successful. This maintains the asymmetric (more upside than downside) payoff profile associated with real options.

Another example can be drawn from Intel, which, in the early 1990s, foresaw future growth possibilities in the graphics and multimedia markets. These computer applications would require massive microprocessing capabilities, which Intel felt it could deliver as long as it continued to upgrade the capacity of its microprocessor chips. While Intel could be reasonably certain that these markets would grow rapidly, it couldn't identify which particular companies, protocols, and standards would ultimately emerge as leaders in this nascent market. Faced with this uncertainty, Intel managed its risk by investing more than $500 million in more than fifty media, Internet, and graphics companies. This was a diversified portfolio of real options. In each, Intel's average investment was a mere $10 million, yet each investment opened up opportunities for much larger upside payoffs.[2]

Hedging

Hedging manages risk by choosing investments with offsetting payoff structures. If one goes bad, another will definitely "go" good. Hedging, unlike diversification, involves locking in a return across several scenarios by choosing a limited number of investments with negatively correlated payoff structures. Hedging locks in a lower return than a well-played bet, but a higher return than a poorly played bet. In financial markets, futures contracts are often used to hedge interest-rate risks.

T-shirt manufacturers and vendors in New York City used hedging strategies to lock in returns during the 2000 Major League Baseball World Series. This "subway series" featured the American League's New York Yankees against the National League's New York Mets in a best-of-seven game series to determine the world champion. The T-shirt companies faced Level 2 uncertainty over which team would win the World

Series, the Mets or the Yankees. One thing though, was certain: Regardless of which team won, its fans would want to purchase T-shirts proclaiming their team to be the "2000 World Series Champion" immediately after the final game ended. In fact, these fans would pay a premium price for such T-shirts, relative to their low manufacturing costs. As a result, T-shirt manufacturers and vendors could afford to stock some T-shirts that proclaimed the Mets as the champion, and some T-shirts that proclaimed the Yankees as the champion. They would make a huge profit on the T-shirts that proclaimed the correct champion (the Yankees), and might even break even on the other T-shirts (after all, they would be limited edition, novelty T-shirts for Mets' fans). In any event, as the Mets' T-shirts became less valuable (because the Yankees won), the Yankees' T-shirts would by necessity become more valuable. This is a textbook example of hedging under Level 2 uncertainty.

Insurance

Insurance manages risk by making investments that are targeted specifically to pay off in worst-case scenarios. Executives hope they will never have to rely on this "strategy insurance," but they sleep better at night knowing it's there. Besides, the best insurance policies really do have a real options payoff structure: Although your regular premiums are usually small, the payoffs can be huge in the otherwise worst-case scenarios. Natural disaster insurance is a good example.

Many contracts feature such insurance. Joint venture and alliance agreements have breakup clauses, for example. Supply agreements have cancellation options. These clauses cost companies during contract negotiations, but they may generate big savings when demand slows or other major market discontinuities occur.

Another form of insurance is provided by investments that run contrary to a company's primary strategy. When some bricks-and-mortar retailers launched early e-commerce sites, for instance, they were thinking more in terms of insurance than really moving away from their traditional storefronts and catalog distribution outlets. These ventures were designed to defend against worst-case scenarios, in which e-commerce would dominate the markets.

Classic diversification, hedging, and insurance, then, are all feasible approaches to manage risk when crafting real strategies under uncertainty. But when are they *advisable?*

RELATION TO SHAPE-OR-ADAPT AND
NOW-OR-LATER CHOICES

Choosing to focus or diversify is not independent of the choice to shape or adapt. Nor is it independent of the choice to act now or later. These three decisions are driven by similar concerns.

There is a clear interdependence between shape-or-adapt choices and risk management. Chapter 3 identified four categories of adapting strategies. Three of these categories are explicitly designed to manage risk. Some manage risk through strategies that simultaneously bet on different future outcomes, as the New York T-shirt vendors did. These provide a *hedge* against uncertainty. Others, like Capital One in credit cards, probe the market through continuous product and service experimentation—a form of risk management through *diversification*. Still others invest in building a flexible organization, such as e-commerce entrepreneurs that built strong general management teams, to *insure* against worst-case market scenarios in which their business models fail.

Some adapters, however, place focused bets that support the market-shaping strategies of others. In the early wars over competing computer operating system standards, for instance, Lotus refused to make its spreadsheet application for the Macintosh platform, thereby backing IBM, Microsoft, and Intel. Similarly, when Compaq introduced the portable computer, it designed it only for the IBM/Microsoft/Intel platform. These were adapter strategies that chose to focus rather than diversify across competing standards.[3]

You would also expect most shapers to focus. For instance, companies like QUALCOMM that attempt to shape industry technology standards must convince other companies that their solution is the *only* one. As I've mentioned earlier, a company that hedges its bets across too many alternatives may not have the credibility to influence others and shape markets. Likewise, risk management strategies may inhibit a shaper's attempt to introduce discontinuous product, service, or business system innovations to a market.

Consider the strategy Federal Express used when it first entered the package delivery industry. The strategy was built around a series of focused bets, rather than optionlike plays. For example, FedEx purchased and retrofitted its own fleet of cargo planes instead of leasing existing models. It built its own pickup and delivery network rather than outsourcing these functions. FedEx recognized that if it leased standard-sized cargo planes, it would have to adhere to restrictive Civil Aeronautics Board regulations. And if it outsourced its local pickups and deliveries, it would dilute its unique FedEx door-to-door brand value to customers.[4] These risk management tactics would have *undermined* the value of FedEx's business system innovation, and made it less likely that its shaping strategy would succeed.

But through insurance and hedging tactics, some shapers *can* manage risk without undermining their strategies. We saw in chapter 3 how Circuit City, by designing a digital videodisk player that could accommodate both DVD and Divx formats, "insured" its Divx strategy. Although its Divx strategy ultimately failed, Circuit City's insurance tactic wasn't to blame.[5] This insurance paid off: Since Divx players accepted DVD formats, they were valuable to consumers even when the Divx strategy failed, and Circuit City avoided having to write off its entire inventory.[6]

These examples show that there is a strong—but not perfect—correlation between shape-or-adapt and focus-or-diversify choices. The same can be said for now-or-later and focus-or-diversify decisions. Companies that choose to diversify (or hedge), for example, often do so to position for more focused, full-scale commitments later on. Similarly, companies that push full-scale commitments to the present (despite uncertainties) are usually making focused bets. Yet those that make preemptive bets may supplement those bets with risk management tactics, and those that postpone commitments may best follow focused strategies.

When a National Football League general manager signs his team's superstar to a long-term contract before the player becomes eligible for free agency, for example, he is making a focused, preemptive bet. Yet the contract he signs will most likely include escape clauses that insure against worst-case scenarios (such as player injury or inappropriate conduct).

If you want to make better focus-or-diversify choices, then, consider first the factors that drive your shape-or-adapt and now-or-later choices. But don't stop there. Since there is a strong—but not perfect—correlation between these choices, other criteria should be taken into account, including the level of residual uncertainty.

THE IMPORTANCE OF RESIDUAL UNCERTAINTY

Uncertainty should clearly influence risk management choices. With no uncertainty, after all, there's no risk—and no need to manage risk. Can we extrapolate this further: Low uncertainty implies low risk and thus limited benefit to managing risk? Not really.

Uncertainty and risk are not the same things. High risk implies that there are large negative consequences to making the wrong strategy choice. High uncertainty means there is a wide range of possible future outcomes. When the best strategy choice is unchanged across a wide range of potential future outcomes, you will have high uncertainty but low risk. Conversely, when the best strategy choice is highly sensitive to small changes in uncertain parameters (like in an all-or-nothing standards war, where a minute product performance differential may make all the difference), you will have low uncertainty but high risk. As you can see, sound risk management decisions require that you first translate uncertainty into risk. Chapter 6 and the appendix identify useful tools, such as scenario planning and decision analysis, for making this translation.

Identifying the level of residual uncertainty and achieving 20/20 foresight is essential to making a correct translation. If you can identify a MECE set of Level 2 outcomes, for example, you can systematically test focused and diversified strategy alternatives against each scenario, and then determine their expected risk-return profiles. Similarly, if you can accurately bound the range of Level 3 outcomes, you can assess the downside risk associated with any given strategy. Since 20/20 foresight provides an analytical basis for making risk management decisions, it allows you to move beyond guesswork.

Developing 20/20 foresight also helps strategists avoid risk management tactics that are of little value. Like the financial planner with inside information, strategists with 20/20 foresight may see low-risk opportunities to focus their strategies that competitors miss. Why buy an insurance policy now, for example, if you are confident that you won't be making any near-term claims?

There are some basic principles, summarized in figure 5-1 and developed more fully in the next section, for making focus-or-diversify choices under each one of the four levels of residual uncertainty.

Level 1

In this case, "no uncertainty, no risk, no risk management" is the right logic. By definition, Level 1 uncertainty implies no risk: The future is

Figure 5-1 Risk Management across the Four Levels of Residual Uncertainty

1 A clear enough future

- Diversification to manage risk is wasteful
- May choose to diversify for reasons other than risk management

2 Alternate futures

- Classic diversification makes little sense
- Hedging and insurance are often valuable risk management tactics:
  - insurance may be viable even when hedging tactics are too expensive
  - shapers must avoid loss-of-influence cost if they are to be successful

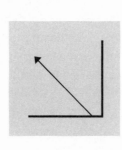

3 A range of futures

- Hedging makes little sense
- Classic diversification and insurance are often valuable:
  - classic diversification involves a portfolio of real options
  - shapers must avoid loss-of-influence cost if they are to be successful

4 True ambiguity

- Risks associated with focused strategies are undoubtedly high, but they cannot be quantified
- Focus only if:
  - unique shaping opportunities
  - ability to limit irreversibility of investments
  - ability to insure against worst-case scenarios
- Classic diversification and insurance are often valuable

predictable enough to identify a clear, focused strategy across the range of potential future outcomes. Building a robust portfolio of strategies to manage risk would be wasteful.

Companies facing Level 1 uncertainty may choose to diversify their strategy portfolios for reasons other than risk management. Some of the factors mentioned previously, such as economies of scope and greater professional development opportunities, may drive such choices.

Level 2

In Level 2 and higher, uncertainty *does* imply risk. The wrong strategy choices may result in significant downside losses. Consider the potential downside losses associated with being on the wrong side of an all-or-nothing industry standards war; of building a chemical plant that fails to meet new, unforeseen environmental regulations; or of being clobbered by an unexpected incumbent-led price war as you enter a new market. Standards wars, regulatory rulings, and competitor behavior are all common sources of Level 2 uncertainty—uncertainty that may bury companies when the wrong outcome in a well-defined, MECE set occurs.

As with most business choices, choosing to manage such risks or not depends on the expected costs and benefits. Under Level 2 uncertainty, the costs of risk management through classic diversification will usually exceed the benefits. Launching a number of random, uncorrelated product and service experiments to manage risk in the face of uncertain Level 2 demand, for instance, makes little sense. If demand levels will be A, B, or C, why not build a strategy instead that tries to shape demand toward A—while simultaneously hedging against B and C? Or, alternatively, develop a strategy that insures against C, which is the worst-case outcome? Hedging and insurance are viable Level 2 risk management approaches, but classic diversification is not.

It is obvious that higher risk means higher benefits to such risk management strategies. But higher risk often also means more costly methods to manage risk. The logic is as follows: If the range of potential outcomes, and thus risk, is high enough, it may be extremely expensive (if not impossible) to insure, and especially hedge against, this risk. To hedge against uncertain, pending environmental regulations, for example, may require an extremely complex strategy: building *two* distinct prototype plants, for instance, each designed to be scaled up if new regulations proved one or the other to be more efficient.

As software companies developed PC applications in the late 1980s, they often found that the benefits to hedging exceeded the costs. Risk was high, as were the benefits of risk management: If a company focused its software development strategy solely on OS/2, for example, and if a competing operating system such as Windows became the industry standard, the company's software business would collapse. The costs to hedge were also acceptable, especially when compared to the environmental regulation case above. In that case, each plant required a unique set of fixed costs; building the second plant was no cheaper than building the first. But for software companies, the incremental costs associated with offering a software product for additional operating system platforms are often not high, since many of the program development costs do not have to be repeated a second time. For many software companies, then, this hedge was a high-benefit, low-cost strategy.

Circuit City, engaged in the DVD versus Divx standards war, also perceived high benefits to risk management: A strategy built solely around the losing standard would result in massive write-offs. It also had a relatively low-cost means to manage risk: Rather than producing both DVD and Divx machines (a relatively expensive hedge), it could create a single player that would accommodate both kinds of disks (less-expensive insurance). This tactic can be generalized: When disruptive new industry standards, new technologies, or new business systems create uncertainty, the range of these Level 2 outcomes is often so great that *hedging* is not cost-effective. In such cases, look for lower-cost methods to *insure* against the worst-case outcomes.

Shapers face one risk management cost that adapters don't face: loss of influence. Shapers, after all, are trying to convince other industry players to adopt new standards, enter or exit markets, lobby collectively for new regulatory structures, and so on. To get the others to rally around their visions of the future, shapers must be credible. Risk management techniques may undermine credibility. Not only do they divert internal resources away from "shaping activities," but they also may cause others to question a shaper's vision. If the shaper is hedging its bets, why shouldn't the rest of the industry follow suit?

QUALCOMM (in the CDMA wireless telephone standards case), for example, was a relatively obscure competitor when it launched its strategy attempting to shape industry standards. Hedging would have undermined its credibility and thus ability to rally others around its new industry standard. Focusing all of its efforts on making CDMA the industry standard was probably the right move for QUALCOMM, even though it was risky.

Level 3

Under Level 2 uncertainty, hedging and insurance are the best risk management strategies. Hedging is a natural for Level 2 situations: If only A or B will occur, a hedging strategy can have some elements that pay off best in A, and others that pay off best in B. In either case, one can lock in a return. But under Level 3 uncertainty, you cannot identify a MECE set of outcomes, and thus you can't develop strategies that have elements designed to hedge against each possible outcome. For this reason, classic diversification—rather than hedging—is more viable under Level 3.

Classic diversification under Level 3 uncertainty involves making a set of option-like investments designed to pay off across the range of uncertain outcomes. Capital One, for instance, manages a portfolio of real options in its credit card business consisting of thousands of product and service experiments that test the viability of various card offers. This portfolio not only *covers* the range of uncertainty; it serves to *lower* it. By experimenting, Capital One gains proprietary information (and thus foresight) that enables a deeper understanding of uncertain, unmet customer needs, and thus it increases the probability that future product and service innovations will be successful. The result? Higher returns *and* lower risk.

Insurance is another useful risk management approach under Level 3 uncertainty. When purchasing new airplanes from Boeing or Airbus, for instance, airlines buy "insurance" that protects them from low consumer demand. If demand for air travel falls short of projections, they have already paid Boeing or Airbus for the right to cancel part of the purchase order. Likewise, many joint ventures in emerging markets include similar escape clauses to manage Level 3 uncertainty.

As in Level 2 situations, you should try to quantify the costs and benefits of such risk management techniques. Given a range of passenger demand estimates, for example, an airline can calculate the probability that it will find itself with an excess supply of airplanes, and how much this excess inventory would cost. These estimates in turn determine how much the option to cancel an airplane order is worth. If Boeing or Airbus offers a cancellation option that costs less than this, the expected benefits of this form of insurance will exceed the costs—and the airline should buy the cancellation option.

As always, shapers must consider the cost of lost influence, a cost that will be incurred to some extent as they try to manage their risk. Monsanto, for example, was faced with a key Level 3 uncertainty as it rolled out its life-sciences strategy: the rate at which farmers would adopt its new genetically engineered seed varieties. This rate, in turn, is highly influenced by consumer acceptance of genetically modified (GM) foods. The recent backlash against GM foods, particularly in Europe, suggests that consumer acceptance is far from a sure thing.

Realizing the need to shape public opinion favorably, Monsanto, DuPont, and other companies that were betting on life sciences may have been loathe to hedge their bets—for fear of undermining the credibility of their claims that GM was *the* safe, environmentally friendly, high-productivity wave of the future. While Monsanto has been criticized for not backing off its strategy in the face of mounting public pressure, Monsanto's commitment is understandable as a shaping tactic.[7] As long as there is still a reasonable chance that the strategy will succeed (and the backlash against GM foods to date in the United States has been contained), risk management costs—particularly the potential loss of influence—may exceed risk management benefits.

Level 4

When bounding the range of possible outcomes is impossible, as in Level 4, risk cannot be quantified. In this circumstance, the costs and benefits of any given risk management strategy cannot be assessed a priori. The risks of any given focused strategy, however, can be assumed to be quite high. Under such circumstances, focusing will only make sense if one or more of the following is true:

- Like Netscape with its Navigator browser, you perceive a unique shaping opportunity, one that can be captured only if you commit credibly to a focused strategy.

- You can limit the irreversibility of your investments. Consider a joint venture instead of an acquisition, for example, or a prototype instead of a full-scale product launch.

- It is possible to *insure* against worst-case scenarios.

Insurance is a viable risk management strategy in Level 4 situations. In the early days of e-commerce, for example, no one could pretend to bound the range of potential outcomes on customer demand, business model sustainability, and so on. Many bricks-and-mortar retailers, however, continued to focus on their offline businesses despite this uncertainty. They were comfortable with this offline focus because they had insured against worst-case scenarios involving lost sales to e-commerce pioneers. For example, companies with active mail-order operations like L.L. Bean owned the assets and capabilities necessary to quickly ramp up e-commerce activity if needed. In addition, these retailers had brand-name strength and the existing customer relationships that might migrate with them into hyperspace.

Companies may also manage Level 4 uncertainty through classic diversification. Of course, you will not be able to tell ahead of time whether your range of options match the range of outcomes. That's why hedging—locking into a return by making investments that are perfectly negatively correlated—is infeasible. But at least you'll have probes in different parts of that space.

Royal Dutch/Shell, for example, diversified its renewable energy strategy under Level 4 uncertainty by commissioning a wide variety of real option plays. This included an initial $25 million investment spread across a biomass project (growing trees for power generation) in Uruguay, as well as a photovoltaic demonstration plant in Holland.[8]

COMPANY-SPECIFIC FACTORS

The level of residual uncertainty is not the only factor determining whether companies should focus or diversify. Others include the objectives of the company, its resources, and its capabilities.

Objectives

If you are risk averse and are saving for retirement, a child's college education, or other long-term goals, a diversified portfolio of financial investments makes sense. This is particularly true if your goal is financial security. On the other hand, if you are risk loving, have shorter-term financial needs, or want to be an overnight Donald Trump, then you'll go for more focused investment bets.

In theory, decision makers in publicly held companies should be risk neutral when making strategy choices (the company's shareholders can diversify their financial portfolios if they are averse to risk and wish to minimize it). In practice, managers of private and publicly held companies alike are not always perfect risk-neutral agents for their investors. As a result, risk-averse management teams prefer diversified strategy portfolios, while risk-loving teams opt for more focused bets.

Similarly, company aspirations drive diversification decisions, just as individual aspirations drive financial investment choices. The best risk managers shoot for an option-like payoff profile, which eliminates the worst-case downside losses while maintaining access to most upside gains. Yet risk management techniques are costly, and as a result diversified portfolios can't offer the upside returns of a well-placed bet. Thus, a company with extremely high performance aspirations—like the investor who wants to be the next Donald Trump—may see focused bets as the only possible means to achieving its goals. This means taking risks. As Netscape cofounder Marc Andreessen once remarked, "If your goal is to create something new and big, you're going to have to do something that everybody else will laugh at."[9]

A company's time horizon for evaluating strategies is also a crucial factor. According to Collins and Porras, visionary companies that are built to last "try a lot of stuff and keep what works."[10] Ari de Geus similarly concluded that diversification is essential if a company wishes to survive over the long term. "To tolerate a variety of life forms within oneself gives a company the resilience to withstand stress and even disaster," he eloquently stated.[11]

When faced with high uncertainty—especially uncertainty caused by disruptive innovation that may fundamentally erode a company's current market position—a company that seeks to remain a market leader over the long haul often must diversify, hedge, or at least insure its bets. Microsoft, for example, is confident that broadband is one of the "next big things" for software and content companies, but it cannot forecast exactly which companies, platforms, and protocols will prevail. Therefore, the software giant has invested in a wide variety of broadband players, acquiring Internet start-ups and taking minority stakes in larger incumbents (such as AT&T). As a result, it has a diversified portfolio of real options to manage uncertainty in the broadband market. "Microsoft seems to be covering the waterfront," notes Jeffrey D. Brody, a partner at Brentwood Venture Capital.[12]

Some companies and their investors, however, evaluate their strategies using much shorter time horizons. Jim Collins, coauthor of *Built to*

Last, notes that many Internet start-ups are "built to flip" (be taken public or acquired) within six to eighteen months.[13] If you are built to flip, your strategy must remain viable within that time frame. Whether you emerge as a market leader five to ten years down the road is largely irrelevant. These shorter time horizons often favor more focused strategies.

Consider KCube, which I first introduced in chapter 4. KCube's goal is to take high-technology start-ups and help them to develop into strong candidates for the next round of funding or an acquisition. At that stage, KCube seeks to coinvest on preferential terms or to cash out.

At one level, KCube's investment strategy looks like a diversification play. It makes small ($.5–5 million), option-like investments in a diverse set of companies. However, upon closer examination, KCube is not trying to cover the broad technology space, but rather it is focusing its investments within a narrow set of related technologies. In fact, it is looking for investments with *positively correlated* returns, not independent returns (as would be the case with a classic diversification strategy).

"Our focus on software companies in related technologies such as wireless and broadband increases our exposure to technological uncertainties," explains Max Michaels. "By investing in complementary technologies we can help accelerate commercialization of each. This focus increases the uncertainty we face, but also increases the value of our portfolio of real options since it increases the upside potential, while maintaining the same limited downside."[14]

KCube's six-to-eighteen-month investment horizon is one reason it follows this focused investment approach. Investment focus helps KCube attract technology entrepreneurs with complementary domain knowledge, as well as passionate and knowledgeable board members and partners. This focus also increases cross-company synergies. Such synergies can be extremely valuable in the highly uncertain product development phase—the phase before the first major round of venture financing. Through this focus, KCube increases the probability that it can keep its companies moving forward during this phase.

Which, if any, of KCube's technology companies create successful industry standards may not be known for several years. But KCube's primary goal is to ensure that its companies—within the next year or two—*have a chance* to set those standards down the road. If they do, the companies will have enormous real option value to their investors, and KCube will earn extraordinary returns. As Michaels puts it, "The payoff patterns from early-stage high technology start-ups are very asymmetric. We will win if we are 80 percent right in 20 percent of our technology choices."[15]

Resources and Capabilities

Diversified financial portfolios are relatively easy to build and maintain. Broad, market-index-based stock mutual funds, for example, allow one to diversify across the leading companies in all major industrial sectors without incurring the costs associated with buying individual shares in each. One fund choice, one transaction cost, and you've bought yourself a reasonably diversified portfolio.

Similarly, mutual funds make it easy to manage a diversified portfolio on an ongoing basis. It's a lot easier to track the performance of a single fund than a diversified portfolio of stocks. And even if you do maintain a diversified portfolio outside of mutual funds, a professional financial advisor might manage your portfolio for a nominal fee.

Unfortunately for business strategists, there are no diversified off-the-shelf "strategy mutual funds" that one can buy to manage uncertainty. Furthermore, a company really can't (or at least shouldn't) outsource ongoing management of a diversified strategy portfolio. Building and maintaining a portfolio of real investments designed to manage risk is much harder than managing a diversified financial portfolio.

Mutual funds allow you to diversify your financial portfolio even when you have limited savings. You can buy a few fund shares and have a small, diversified portfolio, or buy many shares and have a large, diversified portfolio. It may be impossible to build a diversified strategy portfolio, on the other hand, without access to substantial financial and human resources.

A biotech start-up, for instance, may not have the resources necessary to diversify its gene therapy R&D programs across therapeutic areas. It may have to focus initially in only one or two areas. An established market leader like Microsoft, on the other hand, often doesn't face such resource constraints. It could afford to "cover the waterfront" in broadband because it had $20 billion in the bank and a strong management team to fund and manage its diversified strategy portfolio. Such a diversified portfolio is a luxury most new entrants can't afford.

Diversified strategy portfolios must also be actively managed to generate the highest returns (unlike financial investment portfolios where the best strategy is often to "buy and hold"). A diversified pharmaceuticals R&D portfolio, one established to manage uncertainty over drug efficacy and regulatory approvals, for example, will generate high returns only if the outcomes of early-stage research and clinical trials inform timely decisions to shut down less promising investments—and ramp up more promising ones. As uncertainties resolve themselves, some risks disappear, and maintaining investments designed to manage these risks would be wasteful.

It's not easy to manage a diverse strategy portfolio. Chapter 7 provides some helpful frameworks, tools, and concepts for doing so. If these don't mesh with your company's culture and capabilities, then it may be best for you to build its strategies around focused bets—even under high uncertainty.

A final consideration is your company's ability to communicate more complex, diversified strategies to analysts, shareholders, employees, and other key stakeholders. Companies that can't communicate well may have a hard time convincing these stakeholders that their diversification efforts are all part of an integrated strategy under uncertainty. This may create problems both inside and outside the firm.

Even market leaders like Microsoft have had problems communicating strategies with many moving parts. In the late 1980s, for example, trade magazine columnists claimed that Microsoft was adrift and Bill Gates had no strategy. The press also reported that there was tension and infighting inside Microsoft as a result of the competition between teams developing software for different operating system platforms.[16] In the long run, however, Microsoft managed the confusion and reemerged as the market leader. If your company intends to implement diverse strategy portfolios, make sure it has the investor, customer, and employee relations skills to pull it off.

A related point is that companies must ensure that diversification doesn't erode such key intangible assets as brands, reputations, and customer relationships. Every time Amazon.com adds another product line to its e-commerce site, for instance, it decreases one type of risk. But it may increase another. Booming CD sales may help balance any decline in book sales, for instance; on the other hand, an ever-expanding product line could dilute the company's brand name and business model. While there is no simple formula to quantify this trade-off, companies that are aware of it—and think through the relative importance of each risk—will make better focus-or-diversify choices.

FROM FRAMING CHOICES TO MAKING CHOICES

I have now identified the three choices—shape or adapt, now or later, and focus or diversify—that most often bedevil strategists facing high uncertainty. Each involves trade-offs that strategists working in more stable environments rarely face. Such market factors as the presence of first-mover advantages, and such company-specific factors as objectives and capabilities, define the set of solutions available to the strategist. While there is no one uniform solution to these problems, there is a common set of decision-making principles. When rigorously applied to your own choices, these principles can help you manage trade-offs and make better decisions under uncertainty.

A common driver of all three choices is the level of residual uncertainty. The level you face may define what it means to shape an industry, what approach you should take to evaluate big bets versus real options, and what forms of risk management strategies, if any, make sense.

If you want the best chance to succeed under uncertainty, defining the level of residual uncertainty you face and achieving 20/20 foresight is essential. This is going to take some work. Rigorous situation analysis is often required to determine the level of residual uncertainty, frame a set of feasible strategy alternatives, and determine which alternative is best. Standard strategic-planning tools, frameworks, and processes are not up to this task. The toolkit described in chapters 6 and 7, however, contains all you need to craft winning strategies across all four levels of residual uncertainty.

6

NEW TOOLS
AND FRAMEWORKS?

W HEN BUSINESS STRATEGISTS dig into their toolboxes, they generally find a number of promising instruments for the job at hand: SWOT analysis (an analysis of strengths, weaknesses, opportunities, and threats), Porter's Five Forces framework, cost benchmarking, market research, and core competencies diagnostics. The problem is that most of these tools provide just snapshots of strategic opportunities and threats—not the dynamic models of reality that are required in today's tumultuous times. As such, they generate precious little foresight on the strategies that will succeed in highly uncertain times.

Many different tools and frameworks have been touted as *the* prescription to shore up the traditional strategy toolkit. These approaches—such things as scenario planning, real options, and dynamic simulation modeling—have much to offer. But their utility has been oversold. None of them has proven to be uniformly useful across all four levels of residual uncertainty.

No wonder, then, that many strategic-planning staffs are being eliminated, and that those that remain are growing increasingly frustrated with their jobs. Without access to the right tools, they face an impossible, thankless task. It has gotten to the point where executives are deciding to forgo analysis altogether, to avoid wasting their time on analyses that are obviously wrong.

But don't despair: There is a better way. It requires tailoring your strategy toolkit to the level of residual uncertainty you face. This chapter shows you how, as it identifies the tools and frameworks that are particularly relevant for each of the four levels.

Reading this chapter won't make you an expert in any one of these uncertainty tools and frameworks (it would be impossible to provide that level of detail in one book, let alone one chapter). But you will learn to identify the specific tools and frameworks that you should study further, given the level of uncertainty you face when making strategy choices. And in the appendix, you will see an overview of five of the most useful uncertainty tools, complete with references for further study.[1] Reading it should help you on your quest for 20/20 foresight.

LEVEL 1 TOOLKIT

There are three main elements of any strategy development process: situation analysis tools, end products, and decision-making models. Strategy making should always begin with some form of *situation analysis*—a picture of what the world looks like today and what it may look like in the future. The purpose of this analysis is to generate *end products* that facilitate sound strategy choices based in systematic *decision-making models*. This is true regardless of the level of residual uncertainty. But the specific situation analysis tools, end products, and decision-making models that drive successful strategy choices vary widely by level of uncertainty.

Figure 6-1 summarizes these three elements of the strategy development toolkit for those facing Level 1 uncertainty. Traditional situation analysis tools are entirely appropriate in this case. Industry analysis frameworks like Porter's Five Forces provide the checklists for determining the fundamental market forces that are driving current and expected future industry performance.

Underlying each point in such industry analysis checklists is a well-developed set of tools. One might be market research techniques—the focus groups, customer surveys, conjoint analysis, and other advanced statistical techniques that can be used to shed light on expected demand growth rates, price elasticities, the extent of customer loyalty, and how all these may vary across distinct customer segments. Another is industry cost benchmarks, which can be used to estimate the importance of scale and scope economies in the market. A third may be simple SWOT analyses that can help identify likely competitor strategies. These are all standard techniques to analyze business strategy choices from an overall market or industry perspective.

Other frameworks focus on the company's position within the industry. These include company-specific analyses that examine cost structures, technologies, physical and intangible assets, and market relationships. They are helpful in identifying potential sources of competitive advantage, as well as core competencies that can be leveraged in the future. Again, these company-specific strategy diagnostics are well understood and systematically implemented by most business strategists.

It's not surprising that most managers feel extremely comfortable conducting situation analysis in Level 1 situations. After all, these are the tools and frameworks taught in every leading business school program in the world, and applied by the majority of strategy consultants and corporate strategic planners.

Figure 6-1   Level 1 Toolkit

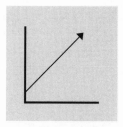

1 A clear enough future

Situation analysis tools	• Traditional tools:
	  – Porter's Five Forces
	  – market research
	  – cost benchmarks
	  – SWOT analysis
	  – core competencies diagnostics
	  – discounted cash flow/NPV valuation models

End products	• Point forecasts of all key value drivers and how each strategy changes them • Discounted cash flow model to value alternate strategies
Decision-making model	• Choose the strategy that maximizes the company's objective

What's the purpose of all this analysis? Regardless of the level of uncertainty, the answer is the same: to generate and evaluate strategy choices. Under Level 1 uncertainty, the end products of situation analysis are point forecasts of all key value drivers that can be used to rigorously evaluate all strategy choices. These forecasts are used to construct discounted cash flow models of future company performance and to simulate the impact of alternative strategy options. The key is to determine how any given strategy—a new plant, new pricing structure, merger or acquisition, market entry decision, and so on—would affect the key value drivers in the model and thus the value of the strategy.

The Level 1 decision-making model is also relatively straightforward: Choose the strategy that analysis predicts will maximize your company's objective. The choice obviously depends on how your company weighs potential financial and nonfinancial objectives, such as shareholder value creation, market share, return on assets or capital employed, employment, and so on. But regardless of objectives, the decision-making process is the same. Translate potential strategies into model assumptions around key drivers and calculate the impact. Then choose the strategy that appears to maximize your objectives.

Even in Level 1 situations, reality is rarely as neat and clean as theory. For example, there will undoubtedly be some residual uncertainty around key value drivers. You'll want to run sensitivity analyses on the payoffs to alternative strategies. But, by definition, in a Level 1 situation these sensitivity analyses, while affecting the *absolute payoff* of any given strategy, will not affect the *relative payoff* of different strategic alternatives. In other words, there will be *payoff uncertainty*, but not *strategic uncertainty*.

The distinction is important, because in Level 1 situations companies will always have a *dominant strategy*—one that is best regardless of how residual uncertainty plays out. With higher levels of residual uncertainty, companies face strategic uncertainty and thus do not have dominant strategies (even if the strategist has a well-specified objective—say, shareholder value maximization—the strategy choice is not clear).

LEVEL 2 TOOLKIT

As one moves to higher levels of residual uncertainty, Level 1's traditional toolkit is not sufficient for sound strategic decision making. Thus, the Level 2 situation analysis toolkit takes the Level 1 tools as its base, and then supplements it with tools and frameworks specifically designed to generate strategic insights in Level 2 situations. Figure 6-2 summarizes this Level 2 toolkit.

Why are the Level 1 tools still useful? They pose the right set of questions and ensure a thorough, systematic analysis is completed, even if that analysis can no longer generate Level 1's point forecasts of the future. For example, Level 1's industry analysis tools ensure that all potential market forces are analyzed, and thus they help determine what can and cannot be known about the future of a market or industry. They provide the checklist for determining key market value drivers. Analyzing each driver in turn allows one to identify those with clear future paths, and those that are residually uncertain.

Level 1's company-specific analyses, on the other hand, determine the strategic implications of industry trends and residual uncertainties for

Figure 6-2 Level 2 Toolkit

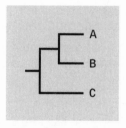

2 Alternate futures

Situation analysis tools	• Traditional tools plus: – decision or event trees – scenario-planning exercises – game theory – decision-tree ROV techniques
End products	• Complete description of a MECE set of scenarios: – industry structure, conduct, and performance in each scenario – dynamic path to each scenario, including trigger events or variables – relative probabilities of each scenario – valuation model for each scenario • Assessment of how each potential strategy changes the probability of each scenario and the payoffs to the company in each scenario
Decision-making model	• Decision analysis

a given company. These analyses show the likely impact of a status quo strategy, as well as the likely payoff from a change in strategy. Industry-level analyses, in general, are most helpful in defining market trends and uncertainties. Company-specific analyses are more helpful in determining the implications of these trends and uncertainties for company strategy. That's why both are important and shouldn't be ignored just because one faces a higher level of uncertainty.

But while Level 1 analysis focuses on generating reliable point forecasts of the future, Level 2 situations require a different set of end products. First, Level 2 situation analysis must lower uncertainty to the extent possible—in other words, distinguish the unknown (can be known with analysis) from the unknowable (can't be known for sure even after the best possible analysis) and thus identify the true level of residual uncertainty.

Determining the level of residual uncertainty also includes distinguishing payoff uncertainty (the payoffs of different strategies depend on the outcome of an uncertain variable) from strategic uncertainty (the best strategy to follow depends on the outcome of an uncertain variable). Strategic uncertainty is what defines the level of residual uncertainty.

Once residual uncertainties are identified, a MECE set of scenarios defined by feasible combinations of the future outcomes of these uncertainties must be developed.[2] In addition, analysis should attempt to identify the probability of each scenario in this MECE set.

Different tools are often required to deliver these Level 2 end products. Decision or event trees, for instance, are often helpful in summarizing Level 2 scenarios. In chapter 4, we used a decision tree (figure 4-1) to summarize the MECE set of scenarios facing Acme as it formulated its pilot store strategy. In that case, it was quite simple: There was only one residual uncertainty—whether Globalco would enter Acme's home market—and two possible scenarios—yes or no. But decision or event trees can also handle much more complex problems, including those with multiple sources of Level 2 uncertainty and multiple decision points.[3]

Scenario-planning exercises can then be used to further develop the implications of each scenario identified in the decision or event tree. The goal of these exercises is to bring each scenario in the decision or event tree to life—fully specifying implications for important aspects of market structure, conduct, and performance. These fully developed scenarios can then be used to evaluate strategy choices: How does each scenario change if we implement a given strategy? What is the payoff of each strategy across each scenario?

Situation analysis should also seek to specify the dynamic path to any one of these scenarios. This requires "rolling back the future" from each scenario. Will change come quickly, say, following a regulatory decision? Or will it be a gradual evolution, as in the establishment of certain technological standards?

The time path is often determined by the nature of the uncertainty itself—for instance, whether it is the result of a single decision or event (regulatory ruling, competitor decision) or a series or sequence of events (adoption rate of new product, service, or technology). This is vital information in Level 2 situations since it determines which market signals or trigger variables should be monitored most closely. As events unfold and the relative probabilities of alternative scenarios change, it is likely that one's strategy will also need to change. I will discuss this further in chapter 7.

Strategists should also attempt to determine the relative probabilities of these different scenarios. In my experience, managers often know more about relative probabilities than they might think. Here's the essence of conversations that I've had on numerous consulting assignments:

> *Me:* We've identified two possible scenarios—A and B. What do you think the probability of A is, given all the analysis we've pulled together on this problem so far?
>
> *Manager:* Who knows? I'm not comfortable making that assessment.
>
> *Me:* OK. Well, I guess we'll just have to assume that there is a 50 percent probability of each.
>
> *Manager:* Oh, no. That's not right. A is definitely higher probability than B.
>
> *Me:* Oh, I see. How about assuming that the probability of A is 90 percent?
>
> *Manager:* That's too high. It's definitely not 90 percent.
>
> *Me:* How about 70 percent?
>
> *Manager:* That's about right. Maybe a little higher.
>
> *Me:* Would you be comfortable assuming that the probability of A is somewhere between 70 percent and 80 percent?
>
> *Manager:* Yes, that sounds right. It's consistent with the analysis we've done.

When it comes to assigning probabilities to different Level 2 scenarios, many managers fall back into their binary view of uncertainty—and throw up their hands. But the analysis pulled together to describe alternate scenarios usually provides insight into the relative probabilities of these scenarios. It will rarely allow you to state "the probability of scenario A is X," because this probability is not a Level 1 uncertainty. However, it will often allow you to bound the range of probabilities, as illustrated above.

In my hypothetical case, the manager claimed he didn't know the probability of A because he couldn't produce a precise forecast. However, he actually knew quite a bit about the probability of A. He knew that A was much more likely than B. And when asked questions that forced him to consider what he really knew about A and B, he was able to narrow down the range of probability for A to 70 to 80 percent.

If one of the key uncertainties is competitive conduct—will competitors enter a market or not, build a plant or not, bid high or bid low—focused competitive intelligence, driven by lessons from *game theory,* might help determine which outcomes are most likely. Game theorists analyze interdependent strategy choices—situations in which *your* best strategy is dependent upon *my* strategy, and vice versa—and help to identify the best strategies for competitors in concentrated markets. In some cases, in fact, game theorists can predict competitive conduct so well that they turn seemingly Level 2 uncertainties into Level 1 predictions.

For example, I have helped numerous clients develop competitive pricing strategies. Often, a key uncertainty is whether a competitor will choose to match the company's new pricing strategy. Game theory analyzes the economic incentives of competitors to match or not. Often, the incentives are clear. In highly price-sensitive markets, such as the one for leisure air travel, competitors know that if they don't match a proposed price cut they will suffer significant market share losses. In such cases, the incentives to match are clear, suggesting that there is no residual uncertainty left after the best possible game theory analysis. What looks like a Level 2 uncertainty—will competitors match my price or not?—is actually a Level 1 uncertainty.

In other cases, game theory can help differentiate payoff uncertainty from strategic uncertainty. Consider Plastico (a fictional name for a real company), owner of a highly profitable specialty chemical business. Chemco (also a fictional name) provided the main raw material to Plastico. Plastico was deciding whether to backward integrate into the raw material business by building a plant that would compete directly with Chemco.

Plastico's management team built a simple economic model to value this potential capacity investment, using market research, cost benchmarks, and capacity and price forecasts to develop fact-based assumptions for key parameters. It found that the data available for forecasting most of these parameters were quite reliable, so that most key value drivers were not residually uncertain. However, one key uncertainty remained: the capacity-expansion plans of Chemco in the raw material business. It was not clear whether Chemco would soon add capacity to the raw material market or not. Plastico appeared to face Level 2 uncertainty over Chemco's capacity-expansion plans.

At first, this uncertainty paralyzed Plastico's management team. It was afraid that it couldn't return its cost of capital on its proposed investment if Chemco also built new capacity, creating an excess supply situation in the market that would be certain to lower prices and margins. However, when the management team used game theory to better identify Chemco's capacity-expansion choices, it found that Plastico's best strategy was independent of these choices. Plastico would in fact earn higher profits if Chemco chose not to add new capacity. However, whether Chemco chose to build or not, Plastico's best strategy was to build its own raw material plant. Game theory showed that Plastico faced payoff uncertainty but not strategic uncertainty—a Level 1 situation that allowed Plastico to move confidently forward with its plant investment strategy.

Level 2 situations may also require special valuation tools, beyond the traditional NPV approach favored in Level 1. For full-commitment, big bet strategies, NPV works fine. For any given full-commitment investment, the only difference between a Level 1 and a Level 2 valuation is that in the Level 2 situation the valuation needs to be repeated for each discrete possible scenario. In other words, different model structures and parameters need to be developed for each scenario (but the valuation method in each scenario would be the same: Projections of future cash flows in that scenario and for any given strategy are discounted back to obtain the NPV of the strategy).

This approach is misleading, however, for partial-commitment real option strategies that build in flexibility (which permits managers to change their strategic direction as the market evolves and uncertainties clarify). Traditional NPV approaches assume that strategic decisions are all-or-nothing, now-or-never commitments that cannot be reversed. This assumption is fine for Level 1 situations. If there is no relevant uncertainty about the future when making a strategic decision, there will be no surprises later that will cause the decision maker to redirect her strategy. When faced with Levels 2–4 uncertainty, however, strategists value the flexibility to reoptimize their strategies as uncertainties resolve themselves over time.

Standard NPV approaches do not incorporate the flexibility of management to reoptimize the strategy on the basis of new information, and as a result they underestimate the value of flexible strategies under Levels 2–4 uncertainty. ROV techniques, on the other hand, are designed to value flexibility under uncertainty. As developed in chapter 4, many ROV techniques are extremely technical (and many are more appropriate for Level 3 uncertainties). But in Level 2 situations, very simple decision-tree approaches (as in the Acme pilot store case) can often provide close approximations—if not exact calculations—of the values of strategies with built-in flexibility.

Once scenarios and their probabilities (or at least a range of probabilities) have been defined, and strategies have been properly valued across each scenario, it's time to make decisions. If you're lucky, you'll find a strategy that is dominant (has the highest payoff) across all scenarios. But this will rarely be the case. How, then, should the strategist choose between strategies with different risk-return profiles across the different scenarios?

Decision analysis provides a useful decision-making model for strategists facing Level 2 uncertainty. Decision analysis allows you to systematically rank strategies with different payoff structures across scenarios. Your attitude toward risk is a key input into any decision analysis. If you are risk neutral, the strategy with the highest expected value across scenarios should be chosen.[4] However, if you are risk averse—or even risk loving—the choice is a bit more complex.

Decision analysis deals with this complexity by introducing the notion of *certainty equivalence*. Certainty equivalence is the amount you would pay to play a given lottery with a well-specified payoff profile.

Suppose you had one strategy that earned 50 in scenario A and 100 in scenario B, and another strategy that earned 70 in either scenario. Furthermore, suppose that each scenario was equally likely. The expected value of the first strategy, then, is 75, and the expected value of the second strategy is 70. If you were risk neutral or risk loving, you would obviously choose the first strategy.

But what if you were risk averse? Which would you prefer? To determine this, ask what your certainty equivalent is for the first strategy. In other words, if you were playing a lottery with this payoff structure, what would you pay for a ticket? If the answer is less than 70, then you would prefer the sure bet second strategy—because it pays out 70 in either scenario.

On the other hand, if your certainty equivalent for the first strategy is greater than 70, in essence you are saying that you believe this strategy is worth more than the sure bet second strategy. The key to decision making in Level 2 situations is using certainty equivalents like this to clarify your own preferences toward strategies with different risk-return profiles.

A word of caution on using decision analysis in Level 2 situations: Avoid the tendency to view the probabilities of different scenarios as independent of (not influenced by) your strategy choices. The relative probability of different future scenarios can be highly dependent on a company's strategy choices; that's what being a shaper is all about. This is an important and often neglected aspect of strategic decision making under Level 2 uncertainty. Therefore, when evaluating the payoff to different strategies across scenarios, you must focus on two questions:

1. What is the payoff to this strategy in each scenario?

2. How does this strategy change the relative probabilities of each scenario?

LEVEL 3 TOOLKIT

Figure 6-3 summarizes the Level 3 toolkit. In many ways, it looks a lot like the Level 2 toolkit. The key end product remains a set of consistent scenarios that describes alternative future outcomes defined by underlying residual uncertainties. And for each scenario, the dynamic path to that outcome should be specified in order to identify the key trigger events or variables to monitor along the way.

Developing a meaningful set of scenarios, however, is less straightforward in Level 3 than in Level 2. Scenarios that describe the extreme points in the range of possible outcomes are often relatively easy to develop, but those in between deliver the most information for current strategic decisions, and they are the hardest to determine.

Level 3 *scenario-planning exercises* are thus quite different from Level 2 scenario-planning exercises. In Level 2, scenarios are defined by the end points of MECE event or decision trees. They represent distinct characterizations of the future, one of which will occur. In Level 3, scenarios are merely plausible descriptions of the future, descriptions that fit within the range of possible outcomes. Since there are no natural distinct scenarios in Level 3, deciding which possible outcomes should be fully developed into alternative scenarios is a real art. But there are a few general rules.

First, develop only a limited number of alternative scenarios; the complexity of juggling more than four or five tends to hinder rather than

Figure 6-3   Level 3 Toolkit

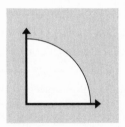

3 A range of futures

Situation analysis tools	• Traditional tools plus:
	  – scenario-planning exercises
	  – game theory
	  – latent demand market research techniques
	  – system dynamics models
	  – ROV techniques based in financial option-pricing models like Black-Scholes

End products	• Complete description of a representative set of scenarios:
	  – industry structure, conduct, and performance in each scenario
	  – dynamic path to each scenario, including trigger events or variables
	  – valuation model for each scenario
	• Assessment of the range of payoffs for all potential strategies across the range of scenario outcomes
	• Assessment of how each strategy affects the likelihood of different points within the range of outcomes

Decision-making model	• Qualitative decision analysis (absent Level 2's quantitative measures such as expected value and certainty equivalence)

facilitate sound decision making. Second, avoid developing redundant scenarios that have no unique implications for strategic decision making. Make sure each scenario offers a distinct picture of the industry's structure, conduct, and performance. Third, develop a set of scenarios that collectively accounts for the *probable* range of future outcomes and not necessarily the entire *possible* range. Many companies, for example, use a *10-90 rule* when developing their extreme scenarios in Level 3 situations. They expect actual conditions to be better than their worst-case scenario 90 percent of the time, but better than their best-case scenario only 10 percent of the time.

In developing these scenarios, Level 1's traditional tools can be quite useful. However, just as in Level 2, these tools are necessary but not sufficient for getting the job done. In particular, game theory will often be required to better characterize residual uncertainty driven by competitive conduct. And standard market research techniques—like customer surveys and focus groups—will have to be supplemented with techniques more suitable for *latent demand* situations.

But if a product or service doesn't exist yet—or you are tapping into or creating an entirely new customer need—how can you determine key market demand characteristics like trial and penetration rates and demand elasticities? Latent demand techniques often rely on reference cases or analogies. When concrete market research data are unobtainable for products or services still in the concept development phase, the history of past, similar product adoption dynamics can often at least bound the range of latent demand.

Level 3 situations may also require a more dynamic approach to situation analysis. Consider the latent demand issue raised above. The demand for a new product or service is often driven by a complex set of market dynamics. These dynamics often feature significant time lags and feedback effects between interrelated variables. For example, targeted, aggressive marketing expenditures may spur early adoption. This early success allows the company to achieve economies of scale more quickly, lowering costs and allowing for more aggressive pricing. This pricing boosts volume again, allowing for further cost reductions and even more competitive pricing.

There is rarely a linear and instant cause-and-effect relationship in a world of Level 3 uncertainty. Instead, value drivers like demand are determined by a complex, nonlinear dynamic—where root causes affect demand through a series of direct and indirect feedback effects (either realized or unrealized) with significant time lags. These nonlinear dynamics can often be simulated using *system dynamics models.* System dynamics is a particularly powerful tool for situation analysis under Level 3 uncertainty, but it can also be useful in some Level 2 situations (especially for understanding the dynamics of all-or-nothing standards wars).

As with Level 2 situations, once scenarios are defined, the next step is to value strategies across these different scenarios. And similar to Level 2, ROV techniques may be necessary to accurately value partial-commitment real option strategies. Indeed, as developed in chapter 4, Level 3's continuous uncertainty often lends itself to ROV techniques based on financial option-pricing models (like Black-Scholes).

The Level 3 decision-making model is also similar to Level 2's decision analysis. But there is a very important difference: Because it is impossible in Level 3 to define a MECE set of scenarios and related probabilities—they are just representative scenarios—it is impossible to calculate the expected value and standard deviation of different strategies. Thus, standard decision analysis frameworks are not as useful in Level 3 as they are in Level 2.

This is a mistake that decision makers will often make in Level 3 situations: They will treat their representative scenarios as a set of collectively exhaustive scenarios, each with an associated probability. This can be quite misleading. Instead, decision makers should keep in mind that the scenarios merely represent a small set of possible outcomes that largely spans the range of plausible outcomes.

Even though these scenarios can't be used to perform traditional decision analyses, they can be used to test the range of payoffs across scenarios. This allows managers to determine how robust different strategies are, and to assess the overall risk-return characteristics of these strategies. And even though a probability can't be assigned to each scenario, companies can assess which representative scenarios become more and less likely based on their own strategy choices.

In essence, Level 3 decision making is equivalent to decision analysis in Level 2, except that it is impossible to translate this information into the standard "summary" measures that facilitate decision making under Level 2 uncertainty—expected value, standard deviation, and certainty equivalence. The logic is the same, but the risk-return trade-offs between strategies in Level 3 situations cannot be fully quantified and reduced to simple decision-making metrics, as they can be under Level 2 uncertainty. Inevitably, despite the rigorous process laid out above, more qualitative "business judgment" factors will play a more prominent role in Level 3 decision making than in Level 2.

LEVEL 4 TOOLKIT

As figure 6-4 summarizes, Level 4 situations require a very different toolkit. Even how one *thinks* about situation analysis in Level 4 differs fundamentally from the mind-set required to analyze strategies under the other three levels of uncertainty. Situation analysis under Level 1 through Level 3 uncertainty focuses on defining the future, or a set or range of possible futures, so as to evaluate potential strategy options against them. In Level 4, this approach doesn't make sense. By definition, Level 4 situations don't allow one to define even the range of potential future outcomes, let alone possible scenarios within this range.

How can you evaluate strategy options against future outcomes if future outcomes can't be defined? The common response is you can't—so people throw up their hands in despair, reject systematic analysis

Figure 6-4   Level 4 Toolkit

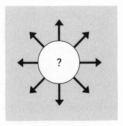

4 True ambiguity

Situation analysis tools
- Working backward to what you would have to believe to support a given strategy:
  - analogies and reference cases
  - management flight simulators

End products
- Complete set of what you would have to believe statements to support different strategies
- Supporting analogies and reference cases
- Key market indicators

Decision-making model
- Getting comfortable with what you would have to believe

altogether, and base their strategies on gut instinct (or even worse, the roll of a die).

But there is a better way. Under Levels 1–3 uncertainty the analyst moves *forward* from situation analysis to implications for strategy. Since this is impossible in Level 4 situations, the alternative is to move *backward* from hypothetical strategies to "what you would have to believe" about the future to support each strategy. For example, if you can't bound the range of demand estimates for a new product or service, you can at least ask what range of demand would be necessary to support a strategy built around such a product launch.

This is a powerful insight, and it is often neglected by strategy analysts. We are so trained to think forward that we neglect the opportunity to work the exercise backward. But in Level 4, this is the only feasible approach to situation analysis.

Once you've worked backward to what you would have to believe to support a given strategy, how can you evaluate those beliefs? There is no analysis you can do to validate those beliefs conclusively one way or another; that's the definition of Level 4. However, *analogies and reference cases* can be useful in assessing whether or not those beliefs seem feasible. If your investment strategy requires consumer adoption rates beyond those observed for any analogous product launch, for example, your strategy may need to be shelved.

Some companies also find *management flight simulators* to be useful tools in understanding market dynamics under Level 4 uncertainty. These computer simulation models, which are sometimes tailored to company-specific issues, allow strategists to test out dozens of assumptions and determine how they drive market dynamics and future scenarios.

No one can be certain whether one set of assumptions is better than another in Level 4. Still, management flight simulators do train strategists' minds to better understand complex interactions among value drivers in the market. In fact, the models sometimes reveal useful analogies to test strategies against—and they also provide a framework for assessing "what you would have to believe" statements.

The end product from these different efforts to work backward and simulate analogous market environments should be a set of "what you would have to believe" statements about different value drivers to support potential strategic actions. This would usually include statements about the size and timing of demand for new products and services, the cost performance of potential new technologies, the form of regulatory and legislative oversight in the market, competitive conduct, and so on. In addition to this set of statements, situation analysis should identify a set of reference cases or analogies to provide a context for evaluating these belief statements.

Working backward delivers another useful product: It identifies the key indicators to track over time in order to determine if a strategy is on course. Strategists can use these indicators to update commitment decisions as they get a better sense of the match between what they initially believed and what the market is telling them.

Given how different situation analysis tools and end products are in Level 4, it should come as no surprise that the decision-making model is also unique. There are no scenarios to test alternative strategies against, and thus no easy methods to make risk-return calculations. Instead, decision making is driven more by a qualitative checklist of key considerations, such as:

- Are the credibility statements (what you would have to believe) really credible, given what can be learned from analogous situations?

- Given the size of the up-front investment required for each strategy, what is the worst possible outcome?

- Are there likely to be real first-mover advantages, or can commitments be staged over time? Can decisions be largely postponed until the situation devolves into a Level 2 or Level 3 problem?

In Level 2, decision analysis quantifies the risk-return trade-offs facing decision makers, while in Level 3 it provides a framework for systematically assessing (if not completely quantifying) these same trade-offs. However, in Level 4 there is no analogous formula or tool for making these assessments. Strategic decision making will revolve around "getting comfortable" with a strategy, given what can and cannot be known about future payoffs at this time. It won't revolve around detailed business cases across scenarios with expected payoffs.

For all four levels of uncertainty, though, remember to use 20/20 foresight. In some cases, 20/20 foresight will deliver fully specified decision analysis, while in others it will merely help illuminate some of the key threats and opportunities associated with a given strategy. In all cases, 20/20 foresight will bring the best information to bear in strategic decision making—even when that information is limited.

USING YOUR TIME WISELY

This chapter has unequivocally argued that analytical rigor is the key to 20/20 foresight. Remember, uncertain times require *more* rigor, not less. These are the times when decision-making shortcuts (like simple trend extrapolations and intuition based on past experiences) are likely to be the most misleading.

But analysis is merely a means to an end. These uncertain times are also competitive times. A "directionally correct" answer available in a week may be preferable to a finely specified, analytical answer available in three months. Strategists must avoid *analysis paralysis.* Realistically judge the amount of time you have to study your strategic alternatives. Just because you only have an hour, a day, a week, or a month to make a decision does not imply that you should abandon an analytical approach. It means you must prioritize your efforts. Even when there is limited time for rigorous analysis, there is always time for systematic, rigorous thinking.

BUILDING AND USING YOUR TOOLKIT

If you've used the wrong-sized screwdriver for a home repair, you know why many business strategists are frustrated with the so-called state-of-the-art strategy tools. There is a remedy, however: Use the four levels framework for choosing the right tools.

Most executives in most industries will face strategy decisions across each of the four levels of residual uncertainty at one time or another. This implies that no company can afford to master only one or two of the four specific toolkits summarized in this chapter: Expertise will be required across all four.[5]

Building this expertise will not be an easy task. Ultimately, all strategists within your company will need to become adept at using several new techniques, and in some cases, even a new language when formulating strategy. More important, they are going to have to *think* about strategy choices in fundamentally different ways depending on the level of residual uncertainty they face. This is the only way they will be able to quickly diagnose and deploy the right toolkit for any given strategic issue. But the rewards to doing so will be great. Once these toolkits become embedded in your organization, you will be able to respond in a rigorous and rapid manner to future opportunities. An investment that promises systematically better choices—in less time—is certainly one worth taking.

7

NEW STRATEGIC-PLANNING AND DECISION-MAKING PROCESSES?

I N HIGHLY UNCERTAIN business environments, change is the only constant. Consumer demand evolves. New technologies, products, and services emerge. Competitors adjust their strategies. New legislation and regulations are imposed.

Some of these changes are incremental and continuous; others are transformational and discontinuous. Some can be anticipated ahead of time, while others come completely out of the blue. But each of these changes creates a strategic fork in the road, at which a company will have to decide to turn one way or the other. In uncertain times, forks appear frequently, and companies that want to succeed must learn how to deal with them.

But how do you know when you are approaching a fork in the road, and how should you decide which way to go when you get there? Yogi Berra once advised, "When you come to a fork in the road, take it."[1] Yogi's advice provides little practical guidance, of course. But at least Yogi recognized that roads *do* fork. Traditional strategic-planning theory and practice, on the other hand, seem to suggest that strategies travel on turnpikes with no forks, no exits, no roadblocks, and no detours—at least during the designated "planning horizon."[2] They assume that the world will continue tomorrow as it did yesterday. But as Yogi also said, "The future ain't what it used to be."[3]

One thing is certain: Managers should abandon—or at least revise—their traditional strategic-planning and decision-making processes. These processes usually run on an internal fiscal calendar cycle, repeating every one to five years, and they are built around trend extrapolations. Key elements of the strategy are reviewed and updated during each cycle. But there is often a reluctance to make major changes, at least for a few years.

In stable, predictable environments, these processes can serve companies well. But in uncertain times, these same processes are confining, and even dangerous, simply because they limit the company's ability to quickly change direction in response to (or in anticipation of) new opportunities or threats. These processes put the company on autopilot, causing it to miss the forks in the road. Eventually, it runs off the road entirely—leaving more agile competitors to maneuver through the hairpin turns of today's uncertain markets.

Are there practical, useful alternatives to traditional planning processes, ones more relevant for Levels 2–4 uncertainty? The short answer is there are many. It would take a multivolume book to adequately address all of them. Therefore, this chapter focuses on a narrower question: As companies approach strategic forks in the road, when and how should they update their strategies? This is an important topic, since even world-class planning processes cannot make a winner out of a company that consistently takes the wrong strategic actions at the wrong time.

I will discuss three distinct, practical approaches for deciding when and how to update business strategies under uncertainty: *contingent road maps, option portfolio management principles,* and *strategic evolution principles.* The best approach for your company depends on the level of residual uncertainty it faces.

CONTINGENT ROAD MAPS

For companies facing Level 2, and sometimes Level 3, uncertainty, a contingent road map is often the best tool. At these levels of uncertainty, strategists can often see changes that may occur in the future, and they may be able to determine how the company should adjust its strategy in response. For instance, how should the company react if its main competitor enters a new market? Or if a major merger or acquisition occurs? Or if industry regulations change? A contingent road map identifies when such contingencies may occur. It describes how to identify these contingencies. And it specifies how to respond to them.

The most effective road maps have these six features:

1. They are built around the contingencies that really matter. There may be dozens of uncertainties in the company's business environment. But only a few of them will have a material impact on the company's strategy. The best road maps focus on changes in these key uncertainties and ignore the others.

2. They are based on a thorough understanding of the residual uncertainty of each key value driver. For Level 2 uncertainties, a MECE set of contingencies is identified. For Level 3 uncertainties, a range of possible outcomes is identified. In either case, contingencies are grounded in facts and represent an exhaustive, integrated description of possible future outcomes. This distinguishes them from contingency plans, which focus only on how to respond to a worst-case scenario in one key value driver.

3. They identify key signals or trigger events for each contingency. The road map identifies the most important indicators to track and signals the alarm when they are triggered.

4. They specify strategic actions for each contingency. Some contingencies may demand a revised strategy, while others may call for maintaining the status quo.

5. They are continuously revised, based on new market and competitive intelligence. Contingent road maps are living documents, not merely scripts for future action.

6. They don't just *recommend* changes in strategy; they *create* changes because they are linked directly to strategic decision-making and capital-allocation processes.

For decision makers who are facing Level 2 residual uncertainty around only one to two key drivers, the contingent road map is a particularly powerful management tool.

Consider Financo (a fictitious name), a financial services company that was losing money on one of its key service lines.[4] The company wanted to raise its prices, but it was uncertain whether a key competitor would follow its lead and also raise prices.

Financo developed this contingent road map: It first leaked the word to analysts and shareholders that it planned to raise prices, in hopes that its competitor would make a preemptive price increase. Financo believed that a price increase by its competitor would be most likely to stick, since the competitor was the market leader.

If the competitor raised prices, so would Financo. If the competitor did not raise prices within two months, however, Financo would unilaterally raise its prices. Furthermore, if the competitor did not match Financo's prices within the following two months, Financo would respond with a deep, targeted price *decrease* in the customer segments that meant most to the competitor.

Financo definitely wanted to raise its prices, but it would not tolerate losing market share if the competitor chose not to follow its lead. If the situation got to this point, Financo decided, it would then start the cycle over again, beginning with analyst and shareholder communications. And in any event, Financo would always follow any price increases led by the competitor.

This simple, clear plan had all the features of a successful strategic road map. It was focused on the key residual uncertainty: competitor conduct. Specific actions were tied directly to observable competitor pricing decisions. And a pricing task force was assigned to implement the contingent road map's strategies—free of other layers of decision-making bureaucracy—to ensure timely response to competitor moves.

Other Level 2 situations also lend themselves to contingent road maps. As airlines experiment with new fare structures, for instance, they often follow contingent road maps that look much like the one Financo used. Chemical and other commodity companies also often develop strategies that are contingent on competitor actions to add or remove capacity from a market.

Road maps can also manage the Level 2 uncertainties driven by potential mergers and acquisitions. U.S. airlines like Delta and Continental Airlines, for instance, should have had road maps specifying how to respond to the proposed mergers between United Airlines and US Airways, and American Airlines and TWA, as these proposed mergers were being assessed by antitrust authorities.

The true-false or multiple-choice nature of Level 2 uncertainties often makes them easiest to track and thus easiest to manage through contingent road maps. But contingent road maps also apply to Level 3 uncertainty. The key here is to determine threshold values for those uncertainties that signal the need for a revised strategy.

Consider Polyco (a fictitious name), a petrochemical company that was developing a new strategy for one of its businesses. The business had historically been unprofitable, and Polyco was considering options to sell or shut down the business. The management team, however, developed a strategy that was capable of generating $100 million of additional annual profit and saving the business.

The plan hinged on adoption of a modified catalyst technology that might improve cost performance and boost revenues through differentiated product development and marketing. Polyco faced three Level 3 uncertainties, though: the technological and commercial success of the new catalyst, the speed of market penetration in differentiated product segments, and the ability to sustain higher profit margins in these segments.

In 1996, Polyco developed a contingent road map around these three uncertainties. If the new catalyst did not achieve threshold technological performance characteristics by the end of the first quarter of 1997, Polyco would sell the business or enter into an alliance with a partner with superior technology. If the catalyst passed this threshold, however, Polyco would continue marketing to differentiated product segments.

A second checkpoint would arrive at the end of 1997: If Polyco had achieved acceptable market penetration by then, it would continue with its new strategy. Otherwise, it would sell the business or form an alliance. A third checkpoint would come at the end of 1998: If competitive conduct had allowed Polyco to maintain threshold profit margins, it would commit to the business by investing substantially in capacity expansion. Otherwise, it would exit the business.

While Polyco's checkpoint dates were identifiable ahead of time, other companies' contingent road maps rely on *early warning systems* to identify key decision points. At Citigroup, for example, former CEO John Reed built an early warning system around threshold values that he called "trip wires." As Reed explained, "If any of those things you set up as a trip wire occurs, you're forced to revise your assumptions. The most important thing is to make sure the world doesn't change without your being aware of it." Like all good road maps, strategic debate and change were tied to the trip wires. Reed noted that the trip wire system "creates an alert management—it forces your managers to be very tightly coupled to the world in which they live."[5]

While contingent road maps may look like an adapter's tool—specifying rules to react to market changes—shapers may also find them beneficial. After all, even shapers have to adjust their strategies as markets shift (just as Microsoft revised its Microsoft Network and Internet Explorer strategies in late 1995 when it realized the staying power of the Internet). Furthermore, contingent road maps—through emphasis on key market signals and focused competitive intelligence—may identify and clarify shaping opportunities that a company might not otherwise pursue. Faster, informed decision making, after all, can open up the first-mover advantages so essential to successful shaping strategies.

A company that faces relatively clean Level 2 or 3 uncertainty—with a limited number of uncertainties and clear resolution paths for those uncertainties over time—will prefer to manage by contingent road map. In such situations, there are only a few possible forks in the road, and it is relatively easy to determine which way to turn at each fork. In messier Level 3 situations, however, it may be much more difficult to update a company's strategy using a contingent road map. New, unexpected forks may suddenly appear, making old contingent road maps obsolete. Under these circumstances, strategists can rely on a set of portfolio management principles to make the right strategy updates at the right time.

OPTION PORTFOLIO MANAGEMENT PRINCIPLES

Companies have already made full-scale commitments to the big bet and no-regrets moves in their strategy portfolios. They can't undo these commitments. They can only revise their plans for future commitments by tracking the latest market information.

Real options, on the other hand, are designed to be "undone." They involve small-scale commitments that limit sunk costs and build flexibility to reinvest, divest, or invest in the future. This flexibility is what makes real options valuable. If a company is not actively managing its portfolio of real options—making the right exercise-or-abandon choices at the right time—this flexibility is worthless.

Chapter 4 identified the six variables that drive real option value and, therefore, the choice between making commitments now or later. As these real option levers change over time, decisions to reinvest, divest, or invest in new options are clarified. The dating example introduced in chapter 4 illustrates how the value of a real option may change over time, driving decisions to exercise, abandon, or extend the option.

Joe and Mary are dating, let's say, and Mary wants to marry Joe. As Joe learns more about his compatibility with Mary (thus lowering uncertainty), his decision to exercise this marriage option will become clear. On the other hand, if Mary sets a marriage deadline (and the duration of the option shortens) or Joe stops enjoying the dates because of the pressure Mary is putting on him (raising the cost of keeping the option open), Joe will be forced into choosing whether to marry Mary—despite his remaining uncertainty about their compatibility as a couple.

Joe's dating option will play out in one of three ways:

1. Uncertainty will decrease to the point that marriage—or a break-up—looks like a no-regrets move, and he will commit one way or the other.

2. Uncertainty will not decrease markedly, but Joe's dating option will run out of time—or become very expensive to maintain. He will then be forced into making a big bet decision.

3. Uncertainty will remain high, but Joe will be able to extend the dating option, delaying the marriage decision until uncertainty decreases—or Mary tells him he's out of time.

Like Joe, business strategists must exercise or abandon their real options that clarify themselves as no-regrets moves over time. In addition, they must exercise their real options when market forces necessitate immediate, big bet commitments. And finally, they must extend and continue to monitor their real options when partial-commitment strategies still make sense.

How should managers make such choices? In two recent *Harvard Business Review* articles, Timothy A. Luehrman develops a simple but powerful framework for updating a company's portfolio of real options

over time.[6] Based on the Black-Scholes option-pricing formula, he shows
that a real option's value is determined by two summary measures:

- *Volatility,* defined as the per-period standard deviation in asset returns
  (uncertainty) multiplied by the square root of the option's time to
  expiration (duration). Obviously, a real option increases in value as
  volatility increases (since higher uncertainty and longer option duration both increase option value). Also, the volatility level of any
  given real option tends to decrease over time (uncertainty and duration lower).

- *Value-to-cost ratio,* defined as the present value of the asset (stock
  price or present value of cash flows) divided by the present value of
  the expenditure required to exercise the option (the exercise price of
  the option at the option's expiration date, discounted back to present
  value using the appropriate risk-free interest rate). Obviously, real
  option value increases with the value-to-cost ratio. Also, the value-to-
  cost ratio tends to decrease over time, since the present value of the
  exercise price increases (the exercise date is sooner). All else equal,
  then, real options lose value relative to full-commitment strategies
  over time (since volatility and value-to-cost ratios both decrease).

Figure 7-1 presents a framework that can be used to characterize and
update your strategy portfolio over time based on Luehrman's volatility
and value-to-cost ratio measures. The framework is split into six regions,
each with a different prescription for whether to exercise, abandon, or
keep open an option.

In region 1, volatility is extremely low, the value-to-cost ratio is
greater than one, and the NPV of an immediate full-commitment investment is greater than zero. In this case, you should exercise the option
and make a full-commitment investment today. The option is in the
money, and the low volatility suggests there is little to be gained by continuing to defer full commitment. Making a full-scale commitment in
region 1 is either a no-regrets move (if the volatility is low because
uncertainty is near zero) or possibly a big bet (if the volatility is low
because the option's duration has run out, yet there still is significant
uncertainty).

For example, if the volatility on Sears's initial forays into e-commerce
becomes near zero, and the e-commerce option appears viable in its own

right, then Sears should ramp up its e-commerce commitments. If the volatility is low because there is very little uncertainty remaining on the profitability of e-commerce ventures, this will be a no-regrets move. If, however, the volatility is low because first-mover advantages will lock Sears out of significant e-commerce opportunities unless it fully commits early, then this will be a big bet. But in either case, a full-commitment investment generates higher expected value at that point than maintaining the partial-commitment approach.

In region 2, volatility is higher, the value-to-cost ratio is greater than one, and the NPV of an immediate full-commitment investment is greater than zero. In this case, the real option should be exercised only if there is a high probability of competitive preemption or if it is very costly to maintain the real option. The higher volatility suggests that it will be a big bet at that time.

Consider a National Basketball Association general manager who is conducting contract negotiations with a star free agent. If the negotiation costs are high, and the NPV is greater than zero, then the general

Figure 7-1 Six-Region Option Portfolio Management Framework

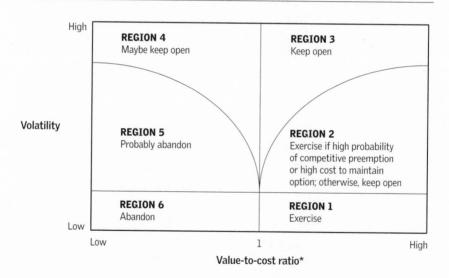

*The NPV of a full-commitment strategy is >0 only in regions 1 and 2.

Source: Adapted and reprinted by permission of **Harvard Business Review.** An exhibit from "Strategy as a Portfolio of Real Options" by Timothy A. Luehrman, September/October 1998. Copyright © 1998 by the President and Fellows of Harvard College, all rights reserved.

manager should commit quickly with a big bet offer to land the star player. On the other hand, if there are insignificant negotiation costs and a limited chance of competitive preemption (no other team is bidding for the player, for instance), then the general manager should keep negotiations open, learn more about the athlete's abilities and attitudes, and *then* make his final decision.

In region 3, volatility is highest, the value-to-cost ratio is greater than one, and the NPV of an immediate full-commitment investment is less than zero. In this case, you would not want to exercise the option since the NPV is less than zero. However, you would want to keep the option open since the high value-to-cost ratio and high volatility suggest there is very high potential upside. For example, BP should buy and maintain licenses on oil blocks with high volatility of potential returns and high value-to-cost ratios even when the expected NPV of immediate block development is negative. These blocks have a high potential upside, and so there is value in acquiring them and holding them in case volume or margin projections for the block become more favorable over time.

In region 4, volatility is highest, the value-to-cost ratio is less than one, and the NPV of an immediate full-commitment investment is less than zero. Again, exercising the option does not make sense in this case. If volatility is high enough, however, you may want to keep the option open even though it is currently out of the money. For example, real options—like pharmaceutical companies' R&D and alliance investments in gene therapy—may currently have negative value-to-cost ratios. Nonetheless, it may not make sense to abandon these options at this time since the extreme volatility associated with these investments (high uncertainty and long duration until option expiration) implies access to potentially huge upside profits.

In region 5, volatility is comparable to region 2 (lower than region 4), the value-to-cost ratio is less than one, and the NPV of an immediate full-commitment investment is less than zero. Since the volatility in region 5 is less than in region 4, it makes less sense to keep the option open, and abandonment is the most likely decision (although volatility isn't low enough to make this a sure bet). For example, many of these gene therapy R&D and alliance real options will reveal themselves as "duds" over time. Lower uncertainty limits the potential upside, so that even partial-commitment strategies will no longer make sense.

In region 6, volatility is extremely low, the value-to-cost ratio is less than one, and the NPV of an immediate full-commitment investment is less than zero. Strategists should obviously abandon any option with this profile. The option is out of the money and has no hope of getting back into the money given the low volatility (low uncertainty and low duration).

This six-region framework is an extremely useful management tool. By updating the value-to-cost ratio, volatility, and NPV calculations for any given strategic investment, managers can place the investment into one of the six regions and get a clear prescription for how to proceed. And, as strategic investment opportunities migrate from one region to another over time, managers can use this tool to reconfigure their strategy portfolios.

For example, an attempt to enter a new market with a full-scale commitment today might show a negative NPV. Still, it may have a high enough volatility to place it in regions 3 or 4, thus warranting a partial-commitment real option approach. The company may enter into a limited joint venture with a market incumbent, for example. Over time, however, the joint venture might issue disappointing news about its market potential. This would lower the volatility and the value-to-cost ratio, shifting the investment opportunity toward regions 5 or 6. In this case, the company should disband the joint venture and get out of the market.

On the other hand, the joint venture might provide favorable news about the market and move the investment opportunity toward regions 1 or 2. If uncertainty at this point is low enough, a full-scale entry into the market may now be a no-regrets move. Or, if uncertainty is still relatively high, but the threat of competitive preemption is increasing (and the company finds this opportunity in region 2), it might choose a big bet full-scale entry strategy.

The six-region framework thus helps strategists decide which commitments—full, partial, or none at all—to make when assembling and updating their strategy portfolios. To get the most out of this framework, strategists should do the following:

- Actively track volatility, value-to-cost ratios, and NPVs for the options already in their portfolios. Investment opportunities will undoubtedly migrate toward different regions over time, as these three variables change. Some options should be kept open, while others should be abandoned or fully exercised. Updating your options in the six-region framework will let you build on the winners and abandon the losers, increasing the overall profitability of your strategy.

• Continuously scan the environment for new opportunities, and analyze them using the six-region framework. The six-region framework will help you assess whether full, partial, or no commitments are called for.

Because the six-region framework is relatively new, I can't offer company testimonials or other evidence suggesting that this is *the* way to manage option portfolios under Level 3 uncertainty. However, many successful companies do use similar option-valuation frameworks.

Merck, for instance, uses option-valuation tools to manage its R&D portfolio under the leadership of chief financial officer Judy Lewent.[7] These option-valuation tools help Merck decide when to ramp up or abandon commitments to new drugs in its R&D pipeline. When positive results in basic research and clinical trial phases move a project toward regions 1 and 2, Merck ramps up its commitment. Poor results in these early drug-development phases, on the other hand, move a project toward regions 5 and 6, and it is shut down.

Enron also uses similar tools. It recently added three gas-fired peaking plants to its portfolio of power generation assets. The plant investments had a negative NPV, but the high volatility of energy prices suggested that building the plants was an in-the-money option. The plants provide the right, but not the obligation, to generate power. By generating power when power demand peaks—during the dog days of summer, for instance—Enron can turn these peaking plants into profitable assets.

In addition, Enron kills its options when they are no longer viable. When regulatory issues made it too difficult for Enron to sell electricity profitably to residential customers in Pennsylvania and California, for example, Enron halted its efforts. In option-valuation terms, "bad news" lowered the volatility of these options and they were no longer in the money (they moved into regions 5 or 6 in the six-region framework). As Enron CEO Jeff Skilling said, "It's like planting seeds. There are a lot of seeds you know are not going to grow up into anything. Our objective is to have a lot of seeds planted."[8]

Venture capitalist KCube also uses a portfolio management framework based on ROV techniques. Since KCube focuses on emerging technologies that often define completely new commercial applications, most of its investments start in region 4 (with high volatility and value-to-cost ratios that are less than one). KCube's goal is to move these investments toward regions 3, 2, and 1 over time. As Max Michaels explains, "In the technology companies that we invest in, the only certainty is negative cash flows in the first six months. The rest is all a real option play. A play on our ability to manage the uncertainties—to attract a good management team, to develop the technology into a product, to find strategic partners, to enlist paying customers, and finally to find the investors willing to assume the remaining uncertainties."[9]

KCube uses quantitative ROV tools and qualitative ROV rules to evaluate and manage its portfolio of investments. It tracks relevant changes in technology, demand and competition on an ongoing basis, reestimates option values, and then uses this information to determine whether to reinvest, sell, or discontinue funding its portfolio businesses.

In many ways, the six-region approach to option management is very similar to the contingent road maps we discussed earlier. They both focus competitive intelligence on key value drivers, and they track specific indicators until they reach threshold values (or move the activity into a different region in the six-region framework). At that time, the company reoptimizes its strategy based on well-specified rules. And they both can be used as qualitative decision-making tools when complete data are unavailable or too expensive to maintain. For example, strategists can often determine whether an activity is in the money by qualitatively assessing the option value levers. Likewise, they can use analysts' opinions, the latest "buzz" emanating from industry gatherings, and other qualitative information when more quantitative data are unavailable.

The nature of the "reoptimization rule" is the primary difference between the two approaches: A contingent road map will precommit to the action that should be taken when indicators reach threshold values; but the six-region approach precommits only to the *formula* that should be used to reoptimize strategy decisions over time. This is a subtle but important distinction.

If a business environment is subject to unexpected shocks—events that are not only impossible to identify in point forecasts, but so unexpected as not even to have appeared on the company's radar screen—then the greater flexibility in the six-region framework can be quite valuable. Precommitment to a formula for decision making allows you to incorporate these new threats and opportunities into your decision-making calculus. Precommitments to specific actions, on the other hand, do not.

STRATEGIC EVOLUTION PRINCIPLES

Whether companies manage by contingent road maps or the six-region framework, they are assuming that the range of potential future outcomes for key value drivers can be identified. But how can companies in Level 4 situations decide when and how to update their business strategies when the range of future outcomes cannot be identified?[10]

Under Level 4 uncertainty, there is no one framework that specifies how companies should monitor and revise their strategies over time. However, there are a set of management principles that, when followed, facilitate sound Level 4 decision making. I call these *strategic evolution principles,* since they enable companies to evolve successfully through Level 4's truly ambiguous business environments. Successful evolution requires companies to be: (a) quick and precise in identifying new threats and opportunities as they emerge, and (b) ready with a set of business principles and organizational norms that will help them make fast decisions and even aggressive commitments despite the high level of residual uncertainty.

Companies can meet these requirements if they follow best practices in four key areas: *scanning, experimenting, monitoring,* and *committing.*

Scanning

Scanning means having a well-developed radar network to collect, communicate, and synthesize market information. Successful Level 4 radar networks have several key elements:

- They are early warning systems. They are designed to identify sources of uncertainty when they still define untapped opportunities. An effective early warning system will position companies to both shape and adapt.

- They involve external stakeholders in the process, including key collaborators, venture capitalists, and even customers.

- They are focused on the periphery of existing businesses, where the largest threats and opportunities are usually first recognized.

- They are never turned off. Scanning is continuous—not just in times of crisis or during calendar-based internal strategic-planning cycles.

Cisco is known for having a particularly effective radar network, one that is built on Cisco's relationships in the world of banking and venture capital. This network helps Cisco learn about companies with interesting new technologies, and it serves as the basis for Cisco's growth-by-acquisition strategy. By May 2000, in fact, Cisco had bought fifty-five companies for a total of $20.4 billion, and it had plans for other future acquisitions.[11]

Similarly, Nortel Networks relies on a "disruptive technologies" team to scan the environment for breakthroughs in fiber optics technology. In one instance, Nortel's team identified Qtera, a company with technology that could send optical signals 2,000 miles without amplification (which was forty times greater than Nortel's existing technology). Realizing that Qtera's technology would be crucial for Nortel's new undersea-fiber business, Nortel quickly bought Qtera. Nortel's ability to scan for the "next best thing" helps explain why a full 60 percent of its $7.8 billion in sales during 2000's second quarter came from products less than eighteen months old.[12]

Philips, another effective scanner, has an international network of R&D labs located in key technology corridors. These labs ensure that the company is always in the midst of ongoing innovation. For example, its Silicon Valley lab alerted headquarters to the early emergence of WebTV technology.

AOL, meanwhile, had its "Greenhouse" group—an internal venture capital team that scanned the Internet, looking for innovative content sites. The Greenhouse identified numerous investment opportunities that led AOL into taking stakes in The Motley Fool and Capital Cities, among others.

Experimenting

Once new opportunities and threats are identified, companies should often develop experiments to learn more about them. When Intel realized the potential demand for microchips with multimedia capabilities, the company invested over $500 million in fifty separate media, Internet, and graphics companies—viewing each as a relatively low-cost experiment.

Likewise, Charles Schwab has always relied on experiments to probe new brokerage opportunities. As Brown and Eisenhardt note, "[Schwab] managers used experimental products such as simplified mutual funds selection and a futures trading program to test new concepts in their traditional discount-brokerage business. In addition, they probed the Internet with a broad range of transaction and information services such as Market Buzz."[13] Of course, not all of Schwab's experiments turned into viable new businesses. But that is the beauty of low-cost experimentation: Even failed experiments provide information and often build capabilities that lead to better future strategy decisions.

Monitoring

Experiments are successful, however, only when they are closely monitored. When Charles Schwab launched its e-schwab experiments, it monitored Web site hits and online trading volume and transaction size on a daily basis. Fast access to reliable data is essential to effective monitoring. That's a primary reason why Cisco is able to experiment so effectively: It sets the standard for real-time data availability, with the ability to close its books with real data (not estimates) in a day—on any day.[14]

Committing

All this scanning, experimenting, and monitoring is useful only if companies ultimately synthesize the information and make decisions—to commit or not to commit. Experimentation alone cannot build sustainable competitive advantage; only commitments to markets, capabilities, and assets create these sorts of advantages. Charles Schwab, for example, eventually committed to its e-schwab venture, and it has become a market leader in online trading.

Companies will make better commitment decisions under Level 4 uncertainty if they institute a number of organizational norms. A shared *worldview* is one such norm. A worldview is a description of how a company expects to create and capture value. Worldviews should be shared by all stakeholders. A shared worldview creates a touchstone to guide strategic decision making in complex, volatile markets.

As Brown and Eisenhardt argue, under high uncertainty a company needs a vision of its own business, and not just a vision of the industry as a whole, to guide strategy.[15] Sun Microsystems's worldview, for instance, is "the network is the computer." This worldview drove Sun's commitment to offer software on a usage basis via the Internet. Philips, meanwhile, has a worldview that seeks to "control the living room space." This statement of intent helped it commit early to WebTV.

Other organizational norms help companies avoid decision paralysis. Companies that set specific, ambitious performance goals are more likely to make commitment decisions when called for. 3M's 30 percent rule—30 percent of sales should be generated from products launched in the past four years—provides a high innovation hurdle that works against decision paralysis.

Decision makers must also have personal goals that are linked directly to the company's higher-level aspirations. Both "carrot" and "stick" motivation techniques work. Some companies cultivate a constant sense of crisis that eliminates any tendencies toward complacency. Intel, Microsoft, and Cisco, for example, are all well known for their paranoia.

Other companies emphasize individual and team accountability— with both upside rewards and downside consequences. Stock options are a preferred motivational tool in many "new economy" companies. Most also have pushed decision-making authority away from stifling corporate bureaucracies. Accountability and opportunity provide the right incentives for managers to scan, experiment, monitor, and commit to new ventures.

Capital One seems particularly adept at putting in place most of these strategic evolution principles. It has used internal "growth opportunity" groups as well as external venture capitalists to continually scan credit card and related financial service businesses for new strategies. It probes these opportunities through experimentation—27,000 distinct product and service experiments in 1998 alone. All of these experiments are rigorously monitored; the company takes great pride in its analytical capabilities. Armed with these rigorous evaluations, Capital One never hesitates to pull the plug on a failed experiment—or to ramp up a successful one.

All commitments must be consistent with Capital One's information-based strategy. The strategy's underlying premise is that Capital One can leverage proprietary information technology, databases, and experimentation to create a "quantum improvement in marketing capability." Opportunities must support "mass customization, delivering the right product to the right customer at the right time and at the right price."[16]

Capital One's 20:20 goal—annual per-share earnings growth and annual return on equity of at least 20 percent—drives a continuous innovation emphasis. And motivation is also maintained through risk-based compensation plans. Most of Capital One's senior managers have swapped up to half of their annual cash bonuses in return for stock options. About 40 percent of the other employees also participate in the stock purchase plan. Chairman and CEO Richard Fairbank and President and Chief Operating Officer Nigel Morris have foregone current compensation completely in return for stock options. Finally, Capital One is known for its liberating, entrepreneurial culture. Power comes from good ideas, not one's place within the bureaucracy. Just ask some of the twenty- and thirty-something entrepreneurs running Capital One businesses.[17]

Companies such as Capital One that adopt these strategic evolution principles can effectively manage and update their strategy portfolios in even the most uncertain markets. They may not have explicit tools like contingent road maps or six-region frameworks to drive their decisions, but they have a clear set of business principles and organizational norms that offer useful guidance.

THREE THINGS ALL COMPANIES MUST DO WELL

As figure 7-2 illustrates, the level of residual uncertainty largely determines which approach your company should use to monitor and update its strategy. But no matter which approach a company follows, it must excel in three vital areas of strategic management: *market- and time-based decision making, focused competitive and market intelligence,* and *efficient internal capital allocations.*

Market- and Time-Based Decision Making

In high-velocity, high-uncertainty business environments, a company cannot afford to suspend decisions until the annual (or even quarterly)

Figure 7-2 Approaches for Monitoring and Updating Strategies Based on the Level of Residual Uncertainty

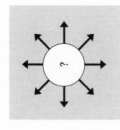

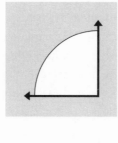

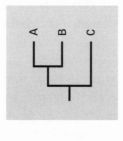

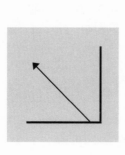

1 A clear enough future

- Traditional strategic-planning and decision-making processes

2 Alternate futures

- Contingent road maps

3 A range of futures

- Contingent road maps (if limited number of uncertainties with clear resolution paths over time)
- Six-region option portfolio management framework

4 True ambiguity

- Strategic evolution principles:
  - scanning
  - experimenting
  - monitoring
  - committing
  - supporting organizational norms

strategic-planning meeting. It must respond before opportunities are captured by competitors or threats become crises. Decisions must be tied explicitly to market-based feedback.

I discussed several examples of market-based decision making earlier. Enron, for example, quickly abandoned its option to compete in California's retail electricity markets when it fell out of the money. And at Capitol One, market data from ongoing experiments trigger immediate decisions to kill or exercise options. These companies do not wait for arbitrary internal strategic-planning calendar dates to update their strategies.

Yet best practice companies don't abandon time or calendar-based planning and decision-making processes altogether. A calendar-based process that operates at roughly the right pace provides companies the opportunity to substantially rethink their strategies at intervals that are in synch with fundamental market change.[18] An e-commerce company will obviously want to do this more often than a mining company. But both companies will want to institute market-based strategy updates to ensure they make the right continuous strategy revisions along the way.

Focused Competitive and Market Intelligence

As a company adopts market-based decision making, it increases its reliance on accurate, timely market and competitive intelligence. In particular, this intelligence must be focused on the variables that really matter: those that determine the success of its strategy.

Unfortunately, many companies don't do this well. Typically, the latest "report" from the company's competitive intelligence group is a twelve-inch-high stack of press releases, industry trade association data, and analysts' reports. There is breadth, but no depth. It's too focused on the past and present—not the future. And, most important, implications for strategic decision making are rarely spelled out. As a result, this so-called intelligence has little impact on a company's decisions as it updates its strategy in uncertain markets.

There is a better way. Whether you use contingent road maps, option portfolio management principles, or strategic evolution principles to manage your strategies, the implications for competitive and market intelligence are the same.

First, identify the key value drivers of your company's strategy. Second, to the extent possible, determine the range of potential outcomes for those drivers. Third, identify the potential early warning signs that would suggest these drivers are headed in one direction or another. Finally, focus your data gathering and other intelligence efforts around these value drivers. These are the data that are most important for updating your strategy over time.

A word of caution: It is possible for intelligence gathering to get *too* focused, causing companies to miss early indicators of next-generation business opportunities and threats. There are ways to avoid this, though. Best practice companies, for instance, also sponsor periodic forums to explore broader trends and indicators that have no immediate impact on today's strategy, but may be vital to tomorrow's strategy. Johnson & Johnson, for example, sponsors "FrameworkS," a periodic scenario-development and discussion exercise that scans the health care field for future opportunities and threats.[19]

Focused competitive and market intelligence is essential to effectively managing and updating a business' current strategy. Broader intelligence-gathering exercises are fundamental to continuing to identify and plan for next-generation opportunities and threats. The masters of uncertainty will make sure they do an adequate amount of both.

Efficient Internal Capital Allocations

As markets evolve, companies must reallocate financial, human, and management "mind share" resources across different projects and fundamental strategic directions. All three of our approaches to manage and update strategies over time rely on the premise that companies will follow through with necessary resource allocations and reallocations when called for.

The six-region framework, for example, may help Merck identify which R&D options are now in and out of the money. But this information won't allow Merck to create and capture more value through its R&D programs unless it redirects resources toward the winners and away from the losers.

Certain organizational norms facilitate efficient internal capital reallocations. For example, companies must cultivate cultures where failure is tolerated when it is driven by uncontrollable market forces and not internal performance. New business ideas and R&D programs fail in rapidly evolving markets, and often no one is to blame. Managers don't fight so hard to keep "dog" projects alive when they know their failure will not keep them from moving on to other vital projects.

It also helps to have fluid "internal labor markets" where winning businesses attract the best talent over time, and losers are abandoned. Gary Hamel, for one, argues that companies must "bring Silicon Valley inside," creating internal capital and resource markets that allow the best ideas to garner the most (and best) resources, and leaving less attractive alternatives to starve due to lack of resources.[20]

20/20 FORESIGHT:
CRAFTING STRATEGY IN AN UNCERTAIN WORLD

Strategy under uncertainty is a dynamic game. Just when you think you've developed *the* strategy for success, a new technology emerges, a new competitor enters, or fickle consumers turn their focus to the next "must have" product. While "sticking to your knitting" is sometimes the key to success in stable markets, turbulent markets require that companies make the right strategy updates at the right time.

Winning business strategies are always forward-looking, seeking to position a company for success in the years to come. One's view of the future a year, a month, and even a day from now will be different than it is today. This has always been true. But the accelerating pace of change in today's business environment ensures that the likely difference between today's view and tomorrow's view is getting bigger all the time.

In this new, more dynamic economy, the deficiencies of the old, static strategic-planning and decision-making processes are clear. It is past time to get serious about strategy under uncertainty. The stakes are too high to continue to rely on strategy tools and frameworks that are obviously inappropriate for the majority of today's strategy decisions. This book offers an alternate path forward.

Figure 7-3 summarizes the book's approach to making, monitoring, and revising strategies under uncertainty. It all starts with 20/20 foresight. Strategists that avoid misleading all-or-nothing views of uncertainty and identify the residual uncertainty they face have the best possible view of the future. This view is essential to crafting and managing winning strategies under uncertainty.

The level of residual uncertainty helps determine which situation analysis tools and frameworks are most useful, which strategies (shape

Figure 7-3 20/20 Foresight: Crafting Strategy in an Uncertain World

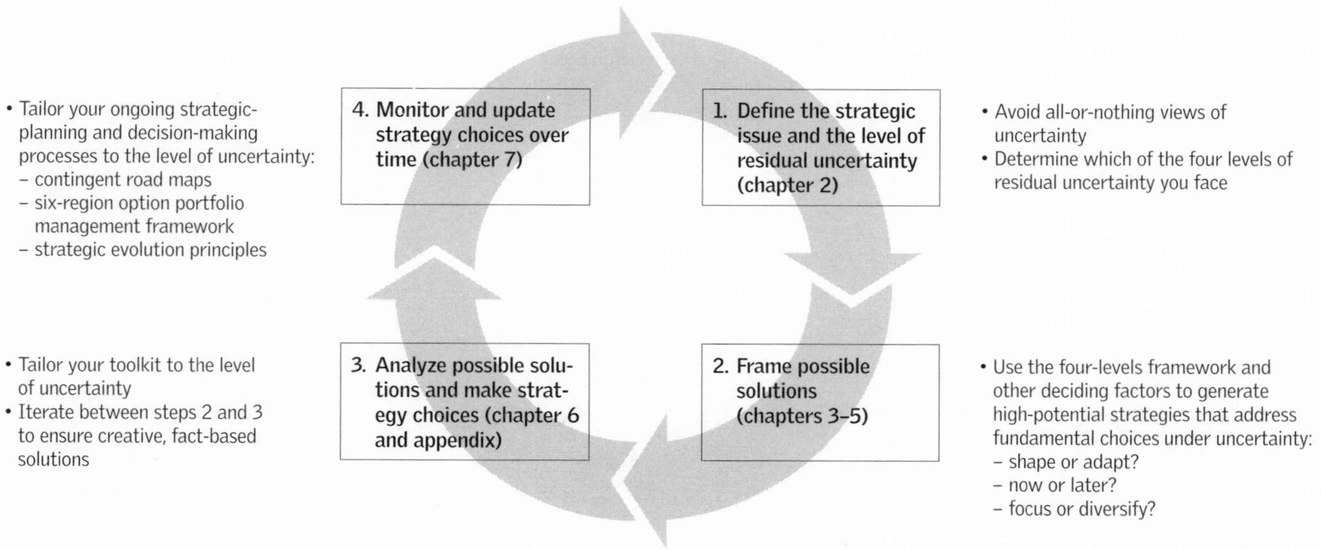

- Avoid all-or-nothing views of uncertainty
- Determine which of the four levels of residual uncertainty you face

- Use the four-levels framework and other deciding factors to generate high-potential strategies that address fundamental choices under uncertainty:
  - shape or adapt?
  - now or later?
  - focus or diversify?

1. Define the strategic issue and the level of residual uncertainty (chapter 2)

2. Frame possible solutions (chapters 3–5)

4. Monitor and update strategy choices over time (chapter 7)

3. Analyze possible solutions and make strategy choices (chapter 6 and appendix)

- Tailor your ongoing strategic-planning and decision-making processes to the level of uncertainty:
  - contingent road maps
  - six-region option portfolio management framework
  - strategic evolution principles

- Tailor your toolkit to the level of uncertainty
- Iterate between steps 2 and 3 to ensure creative, fact-based solutions

or adapt, now or later, focus or diversify) are most likely to succeed, and which management processes are most appropriate for monitoring and revising strategies over time. And when the level of uncertainty changes—as it often does in today's turbulent business environments—the process must repeat itself.

As you craft strategy in your uncertain world, 20/20 foresight should be your goal and the four-levels framework should be your guide. Of that, I am certain.

Appendix:
The Uncertainty Toolkit

CHAPTER 6 summarized the appropriate toolkit for each level of residual uncertainty (see figures 6-1 through 6-4). It identified several tools and frameworks that can be used to develop foresight when faced with high levels of uncertainty. Some of these approaches are well understood. Many (including the entire Level 1 toolkit and such Level 2 tools as decision or event trees) are already being used effectively by business strategists. Other approaches are covered extensively elsewhere in this book (such as ROV techniques in chapters 4 and 7).

This appendix discusses five additional tools. Although they are not developed fully in the first seven chapters of the book, these tools are important elements of the uncertainty toolkit that are not well understood by most business strategists. The five tools are the following:

1. Scenario planning

2. Game theory

3. Decision analysis

4. System dynamics models

5. Management flight simulators

By necessity, this appendix limits itself to a brief overview of these tools, as well as some thoughts on when and how to use them. Its purpose is to raise your awareness of the tools, so that you may decide which tools to study further based on your own interests and needs. To that end, the description of each tool ends with three references for further reading. I encourage you to consult these references. You may also want to attend professional training courses that cover some of these topics in greater detail.

SCENARIO PLANNING

Scenario-planning exercises can be designed to serve two very different purposes. They can be used to help management teams "think outside the box" and question their assumptions about the future. I call these mind-set–shifting exercises. While these exercises rely on facts, heavy emphasis is also placed on the opinions of experts, those who are judged to have long-term vision. The end products are high-level, macroeconomic descriptions of the world, descriptions that help clarify very long-term strategic direction, threats, and opportunities. The scenarios are not tied directly, however, to any near-term strategic decisions.

Mind-set–shifting scenarios can be useful in two different circumstances. First, they may help managers "envision the possible" in chaotic, Level 4 circumstances (although they won't be able to bound the range of possible outcomes and thus are of limited value in making near-term strategy choices). Second, in more stable Level 1–3 environments, mind-set–shifting scenarios may help strategists begin planning for the very long-term future. But again, the implications for near-term strategy choices will be unclear.

The other purpose of scenario-planning exercises can be achieved through decision-driven scenarios, which have a very different goal: to inform and identify a key near-term strategy choice. These scenarios are much more narrowly focused on a handful of uncertain value drivers that drive the decision at hand. The process is also often very data intensive. The end products are scenarios that describe the range of outcomes for this handful of uncertainties. These scenarios are then used to test how robust different strategy alternatives are to the range of potential outcomes.

These decision-driven scenario exercises are most relevant for strategists making choices under Levels 2 and 3 uncertainty.[1] The process is relatively straightforward for Level 2 situations. By definition, in Level 2 you will be able to identify a MECE set of possible future outcomes. In the Acme pilot store case summarized in figure 4-1, for instance, there were two relevant future outcomes: Globalco enters Acme's home market, or Globalco doesn't enter Acme's home market. Scenario-planning exercises in such Level 2 situations amount to:

- specifying key aspects of company and industry structure, conduct, and performance in each possible future outcome;

- assigning probabilities to each outcome, if possible; and

- describing the dynamic path to each of these outcomes.

The first step involves developing the integrated "story" that describes future industry structure, conduct, and performance—and your company's role in it. For example, some of the key questions for Acme in fleshing out the Globalco market entry scenarios would have included the following:

- *Industry structure.* How many warehouse stores would Globalco build, and when would it build them, if it decided to enter Acme's home market? What other retailers would enter and exit the market? How would Globalco's cost structure compare to the cost structures at Acme and other incumbent retailers? How would consumers react to Globalco's store format? How price sensitive would customers be? How strong would the Acme brand be compared to Globalco's brand?

- *Industry conduct.* What marketing and pricing strategy would Globalco use if it entered Acme's home market? How would Acme's competitors respond? Would other retailers choose to change their formats to mimic Globalco? Would there be rounds of consolidation and cost cutting?

- *Industry performance.* How much money would each player make in the market (as expressed by a variety of measures like net income, cash flow, economic profit, ROI, and so on)? How would each player perform in terms of other potential objectives like shareholder value creation and employment?

The industry structure and conduct questions define what needed to be known, or assumed, in each scenario to determine the payoff of the three strategies Acme was considering (maintain status quo, launch a full-scale chain, or build pilot stores). The ultimate goal of such decision-driven scenario exercises is to define the set of future outcomes with enough specificity to enable the analyst to quantify the payoffs of different strategies. If you can't translate the scenario into payoff implications for your company's strategy, you need to build out the scenario further by incorporating the missing (but necessary) trends and uncertainties into your description of the future. If you can translate any given strategy-scenario pair into implications for company payoffs, then you have asked all the right questions in fleshing out your scenarios.

All of this analysis should also shed light on the relative probabilities of different outcomes. If possible, probabilities should be assigned to Level 2, decision-driven scenarios. As argued in chapter 6, simple interviewing techniques can often elicit probability estimates from experts—if they truly understand the set of future possible outcomes in an industry.

Your scenarios will define industry and company performance at a certain point in time—perhaps a natural future equilibrium point. However, scenario-planning exercises must also focus on the path by which the market reaches these different outcomes. If you can't tell an integrated, dynamic story describing how the industry would arrive at one of these scenarios over time, then it is probably not a realistic scenario. Telling the dynamic story for each scenario is essential because it forces you to test the logic of your scenarios. It also identifies the key trigger events or warning signs that, if tracked, may indicate which of these scenarios is becoming more likely over time.

Decision-driven Level 3 scenarios require a slightly different approach. As in Level 2, scenarios should be developed that allow strategists to quantify the payoffs of their sets of proposed strategies, and that are consistent with logical, dynamic paths the market could take. Yet under Level 3 uncertainty, scenarios cannot describe a MECE set of possible future outcomes. Rather, each scenario is merely a plausible description of the future that fits within the broader range of possible outcomes. Therefore, assigning probabilities to scenarios isn't appropriate.

Since there are no obvious possible outcomes in Level 3 situations, it can be difficult to decide which to fully develop into scenarios. The following process helps. First, for the decision at hand, list all important value drivers—those that might possibly differentiate between your strategy choices. Second, determine which are Level 1 variables that can be treated as trends underlying any one of the future scenarios. Third, for the remaining Level 2 and 3 variables, specify the distribution of possible future outcomes for each. Fourth, group variables that determine a common underlying value driver. For instance, there may be three or four uncertainties that will combine to determine total market demand for a new product or service. Similarly, three or four supply-side uncertainties may combine to determine the level of price competition in a market. The key to doing this well is to develop an understanding of the correlations among these uncertainties so that the range of possible outcomes for these more "aggregated" value drivers can be specified accurately.[2]

The aggregated value drivers will thus define a more limited set of variables to build your scenarios around. When developing Level 3 scenarios, some scenario planners choose to focus on only the two most unpredictable and important value drivers. They then build a set of four possible scenarios that "pin the corners" of uncertainty on these two dimensions.

Figure A-1 is an example of this approach.[3] Here, an automaker was contemplating design features for a new car, which would be marketed to first-time buyers. The future price of fuel and the values of consumers were the two key uncertainties. The price of fuel hinged on everything from Middle East politics to federal regulatory strategies. Consumer values, on the other hand, swung on such questions as whether consumers

Figure A-1   Pinning the Corners of Uncertainty: Auto Design Case

Source: Peter Schwartz and James A. Oglivy, "Plotting Your Scenarios," in **Learning from the Future: Competitive Foresight Scenarios,** eds. Liam Fahey and Robert M. Randall (New York: John Wiley & Sons, 1998), 65. This material is used by permission of John Wiley & Sons, Inc.

would adopt "neotraditional values" and thus prefer standard family sedans—or whether they would turn to "inner-directed values," preferring less conventional light trucks, small cars, and hybrid car/van vehicles. These two uncertainties defined four distinct scenarios. Each of the four had a very evocative name—and very different implications for the car's design:

1. Under the *Long Live Detroit* scenario, traditional muscle cars would thrive and traditional brand loyalties would endure.

2. Under *Engineer's Challenge,* there would be increased demand for traditional models with much-improved fuel efficiency.

3. Under *Green Highways,* electric, fuel cell, and hybrid cars would take off.

4. Under *Foreign Competition,* lighter, sportier cars—such as European and Asian imports—would be in high demand.

Developing scenarios that pin the corners on two important uncertainties is just one way to approach Level 3 scenario development. There are many other approaches, but they all tend to follow a few general rules.

• *Develop a limited number of scenarios.* The complexity of juggling more than four or five at a time tends to hinder rather than facilitate sound decision making.

• *Avoid developing redundant scenarios that have no unique implications for decision making.* Make sure each scenario offers a distinct picture of industry structure, conduct, and performance and thus helps inform the risk-return trade-offs associated with different strategies.

• *Develop a set of scenarios that describes the probable range of future outcomes—not the entire possible range.* Extreme scenarios, while possible, often do not help in making near-term decisions. Under Level 3 uncertainty, therefore, many companies use the *10-90 rule:* They develop "best-case scenarios" that they expect to be bested 10 percent of the time, and they develop "worst-case scenarios" that they expect to be bested 90 percent of the time.

Recommended Readings

1. One common scenario-planning method is concisely described by Paul J. H. Schoemaker in "Scenario Planning: A Tool for Strategic Thinking," *Sloan Management Review* 36, no. 2 (Winter 1995): 25–40.

2. For a thorough treatment of different scenario-planning methods, complete with several rich case studies, see Gill Ringwald, *Scenario Planning: Managing for the Future* (Chichester: John Wiley & Sons, 1998).

3. For a comprehensive collection of essays from scenario planning's leading theorists and practitioners, see Liam Fahey and Robert M. Randall, eds., *Learning from the Future: Competitive Foresight Scenarios* (New York: John Wiley & Sons, 1998).

GAME THEORY

Many Level 2 and 3 scenarios are defined by uncertainty around future competitive conduct. Will a competitor add new capacity? Enter or exit a market? Merge with or acquire another player? Maintain current pricing policies or start a price war? This uncertainty matters because most strategy decisions—at least in less than perfectly competitive markets—are interdependent. The best strategy for one company often depends vitally on the related strategy choices made by its competitors, customers, suppliers, and complementary goods and service providers.[4]

Game theory is the study of how strategic decisions are and should be made, given these interdependencies. Its insights are not limited to business strategy. Chess players, for instance, realize that good strategic decisions require an awareness of the likely moves and countermoves of one's opponent. The best chess players will thus study their opponent's approach to the game, and identify the likely sequence of moves that will follow any particular move they make. In essence, they "look forward and reason backward" to determine whether any move they make is likely to drive the game toward a checkmate victory.

Game theory, by laying out a thought process for looking forward and reasoning backward with much greater clarity and confidence, helps business strategists—and chess players—make better strategy choices. To apply game theory to your interdependent strategy issues, you must first define the game you are playing. This requires that you leverage market and competitive intelligence to do the following:

- *Define the strategic issue.* What decision are you trying to make—pricing, capacity, market entry—and how is it related to other strategic decisions being made in the market? For example, if you are trying to make a capacity investment decision, it is vital that you know whether others in the market are also considering market entry, exit, or expansion decisions. Your strategy choices and theirs, after all, are interdependent.

- *Determine the relevant players in the game.* Which players' actions will have the greatest impact on the success of your strategy? Often (and even in relatively fragmented markets) only a few competitors' actions really matter. Furthermore, there are often groups of competitors in a market—new entrants, incumbents, those using technology A, those using technology B, and so on—that have similar economic incentives and tend to act as a group. In either case, this implies that most applied game theory modeling can focus on a small number of players or groups of players. Two to four players is a good number to shoot for.

- *Identify the strategic objectives of each player.* In textbook game theory, it is common to assume rational, long-term profit maximization objectives for the players. However, players in real business games often base their decisions, at least in the short run, on market share, growth, or other criteria. Therefore, you must listen carefully to what other players say, and watch what they do. Public announcements, speeches, press releases, and reports can all provide insight on player objectives, as can interviews with analysts and other industry experts. Talk is cheap, however: Be sure that a player's talk is consistent with its actions. If you reverse-engineer several recent moves by each player, you may be able to back out their true objectives.[5]

- *Identify the potential actions for each player.* For each player in the game, develop a list of actions it might take on the strategic issue at hand. Generate this list from the perspectives of the other players in the game, and not just your own. What options might your competitors be considering, and how will they evaluate those options? Research on competitor resources, assets, and skills, when coupled with role-play exercises involving external experts and your management team, can help generate a realistic set of options for each player.

• *Determine the economics of each competitive conduct scenario.* To this point, you will have identified a set of competitive conduct scenarios. They are of the form "we do X and they do Y" or "we do X and they do Z." Now you must use market information to estimate the payoffs to each player, *depending on its objectives.* For example, if a competitor makes strategy choices based on incremental impact on market share, then the market share implications of each scenario for this player should be calculated. If another player bases choices on the NPV of discounted cash flows, then this is the relevant performance measure for this player.

• *Summarize the game in a payoff matrix.* The payoffs of each player in each competitive conduct scenario should be summarized in a payoff matrix, with each cell in the matrix representing one scenario. This matrix can then be used to determine the likelihood of different scenarios.

To illustrate this thought process and how the payoff matrix can be used to guide interdependent strategy choices, consider a new entrant-versus-incumbent game in the telecommunications industry.[6]

• *Strategic issue.* Digitco was considering entering a telecommunications services market dominated by two incumbent players. If it entered, it would have to choose which service features to offer and what prices to charge. Digitco's only residual uncertainty was the response of the incumbents to Digitco's entry.

• *Players.* Past incumbent behavior and current economic incentives suggested that the incumbents would almost certainly respond with the same strategy if Digitco entered the market. Therefore, the incumbents were modeled as one player. I call this player Analco.

• *Objectives.* Both Digitco and Analco wanted to maximize the NPV of discounted cash flows.

- *Potential actions.* Digitco had four potential strategies: Do not enter the market, enter with a similar offering as the incumbents (high features and high price), enter with low features and low price, or enter aggressively with a high feature service at a much lower price. Digitco used detailed competitive intelligence and role-play exercises to identify three possible Analco strategies: Maintain high features and high price, maintain high features and cut prices, or segment the market by offering both high-feature, high-price services and low-feature, low-price services.

- *Economics.* Market research and cost estimates were used to calculate the payoffs to Digitco and Analco in each competitive conduct scenario.

- *Payoff matrix.* These payoffs are summarized in figure A-2.

Figure A-2   Game Theory Application:
Payoff Matrix for Digitco versus Analco

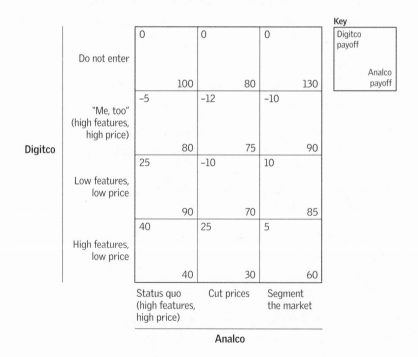

How did Digitco use this payoff matrix to craft its entry strategy? Digitco asked a series of "what if" questions to determine if its entry strategy should be contingent on Analco's likely response. For example, what if Digitco knew Analco was planning to maintain its high-features, high-price strategy? In this case, Digitco's best strategy would be to enter with similar features, but at a lower price (earning 40). The matrix also showed that this would be Digitco's best strategy if it knew Analco was planning to cut its prices (earning 25). However, Digitco's best strategy if it knew that Analco was planning to segment the market would be to enter with low features and a low price (earning 10).

This exercise led to two conclusions. First, Digitco did not have a *dominant* strategy. Rather, its best strategy was contingent on Analco's strategy. Second, two of its strategic options were dominated by others: Regardless of Analco's strategy, it didn't make sense for Digitco not to enter the market, or to enter with a high-features, high-price strategy.

Digitco then repeated this "what if" exercise from Analco's perspective. The payoff matrix showed that Analco did not have a dominant strategy either. Its status quo strategy was best if it knew Digitco planned to enter only the low-features end of the market. On the other hand, if it knew that Digitco wouldn't enter the market, or was planning to enter the high-features end of the market, segmenting the market was its best strategy. One of Analco's strategies was dominated, too: No matter what Digitco did, it didn't make sense for Analco to merely cut prices on its existing high-features service.

Once all dominated strategies were eliminated, Digitco saw that there were only four possible competitive conduct outcomes (two Digitco strategies times two Analco strategies). In this case, the game theory application helped identify a more limited set of Level 2 scenarios, thus greatly simplifying the decision-making process. However, it did not make decision making simple. The problem was that neither player had a dominant strategy. Each had a contingent strategy—and these contingencies were inconsistent with one another. For example, if Digitco thought Analco planned to stick with its status quo strategy, it would want to enter with high features and low prices. But if Analco thought Digitco was going to do this, it would want to segment the market. There is no equilibrium scenario here, one in which each player is content with its strategy given the strategy the other player is following.[7]

Despite the fact that there was no equilibrium outcome to this game, it did provide Digitco with some very compelling strategic insights:

- *It is dangerous to assume status quo competitor behavior.* Before completing this game theory analysis, Digitco was leaning toward the high-feature, low-price entry strategy. It based this on an assumption that Analco would maintain its current strategy, and Digitco would earn 40. However, the matrix showed that Analco would in fact have the incentive to segment the market if Digitco entered in this manner. Digitco's payoffs would end up being 5 instead of 40. The faulty assumption implied an 800 percent overestimate of the expected market value capture for Digitco! You can bet that any executive who promised 40 and delivered 5 would have been sacked in no time.

- *Timing matters.* The calculations and discussion above assume that Analco and Digitco had to simultaneously make and commit to their strategy decisions. But Digitco could choose to move preemptively, or wait until Analco had committed to its strategy. The matrix showed that Digitco should seize the first-mover advantage. Looking forward and reasoning backward, it saw that if it committed first to a low-feature, low-price entry strategy, Analco would choose to maintain its status quo strategy. Digitco would earn 25 in this case. If it led with high features and low prices instead, Analco would segment the market, and Digitco would earn only 5. And if it let Analco move first, Analco would undoubtedly segment the market, leaving Digitco a maximum payoff of 10. By looking forward and reasoning backward, the prescription was clear: Move as quickly as possible to commit to the low-feature, low-price entry strategy.

- *Credibility matters.* Digitco also realized that it had to do more than just announce its low-feature, low-price entry strategy before Analco would commit to its status quo strategy. The matrix showed that a mere announcement would not be credible to Analco. Analco would know that Digitco would like Analco to *believe* that it was entering with low features and low prices, even if it planned to enter with high features. Because if Digitco could get Analco to lock in to its status quo strategy, it could then enter with high features and low prices and earn 40, its highest possible payoff in the game. Realizing this Digitco incentive for "cheap talk" or downright misleading bluffs,

Analco would not find any Digitco announcements of a low-price, low-features strategy convincing until it begin to observe real commitments to this strategy—such as real investments in product development and marketing campaigns.

I have conducted dozens of game theory analyses similar to the Digitco-Analco case, and they have invariably been worth the effort. If you want to start fully leveraging game theory in tackling your own Level 2 strategy problems, keep the following best practices in mind:

1. *Use the six-step process to organize your competitive and market intelligence efforts.* Many business games are more difficult to define and "solve" than the Digitco-Analco case. Some economists even argue that real-world business games are so complex, and their solutions are so sensitive to model assumptions, that game theory is irrelevant for decision making. I disagree. First, there are a surprising number of Level 2 strategy problems that hinge on competitive conduct uncertainty and that can be modeled as simple, quantifiable games. Pricing, capacity management, marketing, new entry, bidding, and contract-design problems have been particularly common in my work at McKinsey. Second, in order to be valuable strategic decision-making tools, game theory applications need not identify unique, robust equilibrium solutions. The six-step process itself— by forcing managers to think explicitly about the incentives and likely moves of other players—can generate breakthrough strategic insights, even when the game cannot be explicitly modeled.

2. *Do not expect equilibrium solutions; in fact, be wary of them.* As skeptical economists often note, the insights one takes out of a real-world game theory application are often highly sensitive to key parameters and assumptions. For that reason, you should run sensitivity analyses around the parameters that are often hardest to identify: the objectives of different players in the game, the transparency of information in the game (are all players likely to perceive the same payoff matrix?), the timing of moves in the game (who will lead and who will follow?), and any Level 2 or Level 3 market uncertainties that drive payoffs in the payoff matrix.

3. *Identify parameters that are driving poor expected outcomes and determine if they can be changed.* While attempting to model the

current industry game, managers invariably develop insights on how to change the game to drive more favorable outcomes. Unlike games like chess, in business games the rules, players, and potential moves are not given. Thus, while game theory can help you play your current game better, its greatest value often comes from helping you define new games. For example, I have seen several game theory applications where the initial conclusion was that the industry was ripe for a price war (because customers were extremely price sensitive in making purchasing decisions). This price sensitivity was giving each of the major producers an economic incentive to undercut its competitor's price. Game-theory modeling, by identifying the root cause of price war dynamics, also identified potential methods to change the game: Customer loyalty programs and product differentiation were just two ideas that might create value for customers and producers while decreasing the incentives for destructive price competition. If you do not periodically change the game to gain competitive advantage, you can bet one of your competitors will. And there is not much value in being the best chess player in town when everyone else is playing checkers.

Lessons about game theory under Level 2 uncertainty are also applicable to game theory applications when there is Level 3 uncertainty over competitive conduct. However, a payoff matrix is no longer used to summarize the game, since there is no MECE set of distinct competitor strategies available to define its cells. In this case, the game is summarized by *reaction functions* that specify the best strategic response of one player to the range of possible actions of another player. When faced with continuous Level 3 uncertainty over Pepsi's pricing strategy, for example, Coke can develop a reaction function that specifies its best price for any given Pepsi price—and vice versa, of course. For more on reaction functions, consult any intermediate game theory textbook.

Recommended Readings

1. For a thorough, accessible introduction to applied game theory, see Avinash K. Dixit and Barry J. Nalebuff, *Thinking Strategically: The*

Competitive Edge in Business, Politics, and Everyday Life (New York: W. W. Norton & Company, 1991).

2. For more on how to think like a game theorist when crafting business strategy (as opposed to relying on formal game theory modeling), see Adam J. Brandenburger and Barry J. Nalebuff, *Co-opetition* (New York: Currency Doubleday, 1996).

3. For a more formal treatment that demonstrates how mathematical game theory models can be applied to business cases, see Pankaj Ghemawat, *Games Businesses Play: Cases and Models* (Cambridge: MIT Press, 1997).

DECISION ANALYSIS

You are facing Level 2 or Level 3 uncertainty, and you have developed a list of possible strategies and valued them across a set of future scenarios. Your strategies will now probably show varied payoff profiles. Some might perform extremely well in some scenarios, but lead to bankruptcy in others. Others might generate a steady stream of payoffs, but prevent you from reaching stretch growth goals. Given these payoff profiles, how should you decide between different strategies?

Decision analysis is a methodology and set of tools for facilitating sound decision making under Levels 2 and 3 uncertainty. The decision analysis toolkit is quite broad, consisting of many different approaches that can be tailored to the exact situation.[8] All the approaches, however, emphasize how to make systematic, logical choices given the following:

- Alternatives (your set of potential strategies)

- Potential outcomes (how these strategies might play out given residual uncertainty)

- Probabilities of potential outcomes

- Objectives (in particular, your attitude toward risk)

Consider Flexor (a fictitious name), a supplier of high-performance plastics to the automotive, aerospace, and other transport industries, which used decision analysis techniques to guide its strategy choices when faced with Level 2 uncertainty.[9] Because its plastics were essential to safety, Flexor's production processes were tightly regulated by government authorities. As a result, all the incumbent producers in the industry had adopted a standard process technology.

Two competitors, however, were poised to enter the industry. Each was touting a new process technology that it claimed offered significant cost and performance advantages. And each expected industry regulators to designate its technology as the new standard for the industry.

It seemed likely that one, but not both, of the new technologies would become the new industry standard, and that incumbent players would have to adopt this standard to earn acceptable returns. Flexor and the other incumbents faced Level 2 uncertainty: Which new technology, A or B, would become the industry standard?

Each new entrant wanted its technology to become the industry standard, of course, and thus each offered the incumbents a technology license. Flexor had to choose between four strategies: Maintain its status quo strategy; sell its business to another incumbent (it had an offer on the table for 80); license technology A and begin building new plants and retrofitting old plants to use it; license technology B and begin building new plants and retrofitting old plants to use it.

Using detailed analysis of the impact on investment costs, ongoing cash costs, prices, and expected future market shares for each of the producers, Flexor calculated the expected payoffs of each of these strategies if technology A became the standard and if technology B became the standard. Table A-1 presents these payoffs.

How should Flexor choose between these four strategies? Once the payoffs have been estimated, as in table A-1, the answer depends on the objectives of the decision maker.[10] The most straightforward decision-making rule is *outcome dominance.* Is there a dominant strategy, with the

Table A-1   Flexor's Strategy Alternatives and Payoffs

	SCENARIO PAYOFFS	
Strategy	Technology A Becomes Standard	Technology B Becomes Standard
1. Maintain status quo	60	75
2. Sell the business	80	80
3. License technology A	70	50
4. License technology B	40	100

highest payoff in both scenarios A and B? In Flexor's case, no. Selling the business for 80 dominates two of the strategies—maintaining the status quo and licensing technology A—but it does not dominate licensing technology B. While there is no dominant strategy in this case, checking for dominance should always be the first step in your decision-making process.

Absent a dominant strategy, what should Flexor do? If Flexor is most interested in protecting against downside losses, it might choose the *maximin* strategy. The maximin strategy is the one that maximizes the value of the worst possible payoff across the two scenarios. In other words, it has the best possible downside. The maximin strategy in this case would be to sell the business for 80.

But suppose that Flexor is most interested in capturing the highest upside opportunity afforded by the new technologies. In this case, it might choose the *maximax* strategy—the strategy with the highest upside payoff. In this case, the maximax strategy is to license technology B.

A third possibility is that Flexor wants to ensure that its strategy looks best in hindsight. In this case, the *minimax regret* strategy might be chosen. Regret in this context is measured by the highest possible payoff in a scenario—if you had chosen the best strategy—minus the payoff you receive with an alternative strategy. If technology A becomes the industry standard (scenario A), the highest possible payoff is 80, while if technology B becomes the industry standard (scenario B), the highest possible payoff is 100. Table A-2 shows the regret associated with each strategy. The strategy with minimax regret is the one with the smallest maximum regret across the two scenarios. It is the strategy where in the worst case you are closest to the maximum payoff, and thus unlikely to incur the wrath of investors who may evaluate your strategy later with the benefit of 20/20 hindsight. In this case, the minimax regret strategy is to sell the business.

Table A–2   Flexor's Minimax Regret Strategy

	SCENARIO REGRET		
Strategy	**Technology A Becomes Standard**	**Technology B Becomes Standard**	
1. Maintain status quo	20	25	
2. Sell the business	0	20	Minimax regret strategy
3. License technology A	10	50	
4. License technology B	40	0	

All of the decision-making criteria discussed above can be applied without relying on estimates of the probability of each scenario. This is good news, since it's not always possible to estimate such probabilities, even in the most straightforward Level 2 situations. However, as argued in chapter 6, even when precise estimates of probabilities are not possible, probability ranges can often be identified. In addition, strategists can work backward from payoffs to what you would have to believe about probabilities to choose one strategy over another.

If probability estimates are available, how should they guide Level 2 decision making? The probabilities for Flexor's scenarios A and B are shown in table A-3. Scenario A and B probabilities are *not independent* of Flexor's strategy choice. If Flexor licenses either of the new technologies, that technology is more likely to become the new industry standard. Using the terminology from chapter 3, Flexor can choose a shaper strategy that *influences* future industry technology standards (although it does not have the clout to *determine* the standard through its strategy). When evaluating the expected payoff of a given strategy you must focus both on the impact it has on the probability of each scenario and on the impact it has on payoffs in each scenario.

Once probability estimates for each scenario-strategy combination are available, Flexor's attitude toward risk is the key determinant in deciding which strategy to implement. If Flexor is risk neutral, then it should base its decision on the expected value of payoffs.[11] In this case, licensing technology B returns the highest expected value, 82. If Flexor wasn't confident that its probability estimates were precise, it could work backward to determine what it would have to believe to license technology B instead of selling the business. Working backward, it is easy to show that as long as the probability of scenario B is 67 percent or higher, licensing technology B has the highest expected value.[12]

When decision makers are either risk averse or risk seeking, simple expected value calculations can be misleading. As introduced in chapter 6, decision analysis uses the certainty equivalence concept to guide decision making for risk-averse or risk-seeking strategists. Certainty equivalence is the amount you would pay to play a given lottery with a well-specified payoff profile.

The Flexor status quo strategy "lottery" pays off either 60 or 75, with each outcome equally likely. The expected value of the lottery is 67.5. This is also the certainty equivalent for a risk-neutral strategist. Flexor's

Table A–3 Flexor's Strategy Alternatives and Payoffs: Using Probabilities

Strategy	SCENARIO PAYOFFS		SCENARIO PROBABILITIES		Expected Value	Certainty Equivalent	
	Technology A Becomes Standard	Technology B Becomes Standard	Technology A Becomes Standard	Technology B Becomes Standard			
1. Maintain status quo	60	75	.5	.5	67.5	65	
2. Sell the business	80	80	.5	.5	80	80	Risk-averse strategy
3. License technology A	70	50	.7	.3	64	60	
4. License technology B	40	100	.3	.7	82	70	Risk-neutral strategy

decision makers, however, were risk averse. As a result, they focused on the downside payoff of 60, and thus they were not willing to pay the full expected value to play this lottery. Their certainty equivalence for the status quo strategy was 65. Likewise, they were only willing to pay 70 to play the technology B licensing strategy lottery despite its high expected value of 82. This strategy had a 30 percent chance of paying off only 40—and that was the reason that Flexor's risk-averse managers discounted the expected value so significantly when determining the strategy's certainty equivalent. With risk-averse decision makers like these, certainty equivalents showed that Flexor was better off taking the "sure bet" (selling the business) despite the fact that licensing technology B had a higher expected value.[13]

As the Flexor case illustrates, strategy choices under uncertainty are rarely dominant across all possible management objectives. As a result, most management teams would benefit from spending more time up-front discussing their decision-making criteria and levels of risk aversion. Many teams never explicitly address these issues, resulting in decision-making confusion and paralysis that prevents them from moving aggressively ahead with bold, shaping strategies.

While the Flexor case illustrated a Level 2 application of decision analysis, it is obvious that many of the same tools and concepts are applicable to Level 3 situations as well. Level 3 scenarios can be specified, and payoffs of different strategies in each scenario can be quantified. One can then search for strategies that might be dominant across scenarios, or absent dominance, meet some other decision-making criterion like minimax regret. But, as chapter 6 argued, one can take this analysis only so far.

The problem is that it is usually impossible to define a MECE set of scenarios and related probabilities under Level 3 uncertainty. The best one can do is identify a representative set of outcomes. This implies that a strategy that is shown to be dominant across the range of representative outcomes—or maximizes some other decision-making criterion across these scenarios—may not be the best choice after all. Furthermore, such measures as expected value and certainty equivalence (which require scenario probabilities to calculate) cannot be quantified.

Still, if you choose your representative scenarios wisely—so that they cover the probable range of outcomes—they can be used to test the range of payoffs across scenarios. This allows managers to determine how robust different strategies are, and to assess the high-level risk-return characteristics of these strategies. This more qualitative approach to decision analysis can still provide great insight when crafting strategy choices under Level 3 uncertainty.[14]

Recommended Readings

1. For a thorough, advanced undergraduate textbook treatment of decision analysis, see Robert T. Clemen, *Making Hard Decisions: An Introduction to Decision Analysis,* 2nd ed. (Pacific Grove, CA: Duxbury Press, 1996).

2. For a practitioner's guide to the field, see David C. Skinner, *Introduction to Decision Analysis: A Practitioner's Guide to Improving Decision Quality,* 2nd ed. (Gainesville, FL: Probabilistic Publishing, 1999).

3. For a managerial guide to decision-making biases and how to avoid them, see J. Edward Russo and Paul J. H. Schoemaker, *Decision Traps: The Ten Barriers to Brilliant Decision-Making and How to Overcome Them* (New York: Doubleday, 1989).

SYSTEM DYNAMICS MODELS

The relationship between cause and effect is extremely complex in most business environments, and for at least the two following reasons, it is difficult to estimate:

- *Feedback effects.* One action can set off other actions that either reinforce or counteract (balance) the original action. These indirect feedback effects often make it very difficult to ascertain the ultimate impact—either prospectively or retrospectively—of the original action.

- *Time delays.* There are often significant time delays between when an action is taken and its impact is felt. This makes it difficult to separate out the impact of the original action from other subsequent actions that occur during the time delay period.

With reinforcing feedback effects, small actions can grow into large consequences. This feedback causes either accelerating growth or accelerating decline. For example, a law firm that is growing quickly creates greater promotion opportunities, which increases associate morale, which leads to higher motivation and productivity. These elements, in turn, lead to higher-impact client service, which creates even more business opportunities and higher growth.

But this growth is naturally checked by balancing feedback effects. These tend to create stability in a system that otherwise might be on the path of accelerating growth or decline. Balancing feedback occurs naturally whenever there is management by explicit strategy or goals. For example, while a law firm may have no explicit growth goals, it may have determined the kind of cases it wants to take. It may not take tax cases, for instance. This decision naturally constrains the firm's growth.

In addition, there would undoubtedly be balancing feedback effects beyond its strategy that would limit the firm's growth. If it grew too fast, for instance, the quality of its incoming associate pool would decrease, as would the ratio of partners and senior associates relative to newcomers. Less coaching and mentoring opportunities would be available; the quality of the firm's work would suffer; client demand for its services would slow; morale and productivity would decrease, and so on, until a more sustainable rate of growth was achieved.

Obviously, there is an extremely complex set of reinforcing and balancing feedback effects, most with significant time delays, that influence the law firm's sustainable growth rate. Suppose you were the firm's managing partner, and you were tasked with setting such fundamental human resource policies as new associate compensation, average and range of years to partner election, the ratio of salary to bonus, hiring targets, and the content of training programs. Given feedback effects and time delays, the link between these changes and their potential impact on morale, productivity, client impact, growth, and associate and client retention would be extremely hard to assess. How could you make more informed commitments on these choices—which may involve millions of dollars of upfront investments as well as the risk of upsetting certain aspects of your firm's culture—despite this uncertainty over cause and effect?

System dynamics modeling is a tool that may help you craft an answer. The first step in developing a system dynamics model is to fully specify the reinforcing and balancing feedback effects, as well as time delays, that influence the issue at hand. A graphical representation of these effects is called a *causal map.*

Figure A-3, for example, is a causal map developed by a financial services firm to help it understand the relationship between human

Figure A-3 Causal Map: Director Capacity and Firm Performance

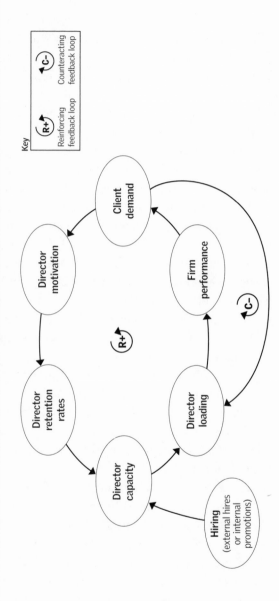

Source: This figure was originally published in **The McKinsey Quarterly** 2000 no. 1, 106–115. Copyright © 2000 McKinsey & Company. All rights reserved. Reprinted by permission.

resource policies, firm talent, and growth.[15] By clarifying the feedback effects, the map forces viewers to consider all of the direct and indirect effects of any policy changes. Setting the optimal "loading" of senior directors (clients per director), for example, is key to sustaining profitable growth. The right load gives directors the right amount of time to serve old clients well and develop new ones. As a result, client service levels improve, which in turn increases the firm's reputation, its client demand, and profitability. As director compensation grows, more directors are retained. In the end, growth draws more talented people into the firm, further improving client service, demand, and remuneration. On the other hand, as director loads become too high, client service levels, client demand, and director compensation and retention all head south.

If enough information is available to quantify these feedback effects (for instance, "a 1 percent increase in the firm's client demand increases director compensation and retention rates by 0.5 percent") then the issue can be simulated using a system dynamics model. In essence, a system dynamics model is a series of differential equations that describes how variables in the system are related, and how they change over time when there are any shocks to the system like a new human resources policy. The model quantifies relationships depicted in a causal map, and by doing so it allows for a more quantitative, precise description of the dynamics set off by any changes to the system.

While the idea of building a model based on a system of differential equations may not strike you as a very easy thing to do, there are a number of software packages (including Vensim and ithink) that can turn any causal map into a system dynamics simulation model.[16] If you can draw and describe the system quantitatively, in other words, these packages can build your simulation model.

In the financial services case, for instance, the firm used its causal maps to create a system dynamics model that simulated potential human resource policy changes. Some of the results were striking. It found, for example, that its most senior directors should spend *no time* coaching apprentices, but rather they should spend their time on client work, which would improve the firm's financial performance and in turn attract the best recruits (who could then be trained by more junior members of the firm).

System dynamics models can deliver similarly useful insights for decision makers facing a wide variety of Level 2, and particularly Level 3, uncertainties. They may, for example, help bound the range of possible outcomes when there is uncertainty around the performance attributes and customer adoption rates of new products and technologies. In the process, they can also help identify the key trigger events or variables that will largely determine where within the range the final outcome will occur.

A system dynamics model, for example, was used to simulate future demand scenarios for European landline and mobile telephone service.[17] The model was able to put confident bounds on two important, uncertain parameters: Almost all of the scenarios suggested that between 65 and 75 percent of European residential voice traffic would travel over mobile networks within three to five years, and 35 to 45 percent of European consumers would give up their landline service unless fixed monthly charges were eliminated. The model also identified a key trigger variable to track: mobile operator pricing strategies. If mobile operators priced aggressively, for instance, there would be a more rapid decline in land-line voice traffic.

System dynamics models can also help quantify the network externality effects—first introduced in chapter 2—that drive all-or-nothing Level 2 standards wars. For example, they might help quantify the number and type of end users that would have to adopt Linux or Unix before either had any hope of displacing Windows as the PC operating system standard.

As the examples above illustrate, system dynamics models can be very beneficial when crafting strategies under Levels 2 and 3 uncertainty. However, these benefits do come at a cost. It can take a team of two to three analysts up to six to eight weeks to construct, test, and analyze a fully specified model, even given user-friendly simulation packages like Vensim and ithink. When is it worth the effort?

When you face an issue with dynamic complexity—featuring significant time delays and feedback effects—taking the initial step to draw out a causal map is a no-regrets move. The map itself might generate new strategic insights. At that time, however, you should reassess the need for more complete simulation modeling. What incremental insight is likely to come out of the model, and how much time will be required? Ask yourself what the model would have to demonstrate to change your initial hypothesis on strategic direction. How important would these feedback effects have to be, and are effects of that magnitude feasible?

If your needs pass these initial criteria, build a simple, "straw man" simulation model using one of the previously mentioned software packages. But before adding any further complexity to the model, ensure that incremental insight is likely to come out of this effort.

In crafting your final strategy recommendations, combine your simulation model results with other lower-tech analyses and business intuition. System dynamics models, after all, are not a substitute for the rest of your strategy toolkit.

Recommended Readings

1. For a thorough textbook treatment of the system dynamics field, see John D. Sterman, *Business Dynamics: Systems Thinking and Modeling for a Complex World* (Columbus, OH: McGraw-Hill/Irwin, 2000).

2. For insights on how to apply and embed systems thinking within organizations, see Peter M. Senge, *The Fifth Discipline: The Art and Practice of the Learning Organization* (New York: Currency Doubleday, 1994).

3. For several applications of system dynamics concepts and models to business strategy issues, see the articles in *Business Dynamics: Overcoming the Limits to Growth, The McKinsey Quarterly Anthologies* (New York: McKinsey & Company, 1998).

MANAGEMENT FLIGHT SIMULATORS

Management flight simulators—also known as microworlds—are computer-based simulation games that are driven by system dynamics models. These simulators allow managers to practice making strategy in dynamically complex industry environments featuring multiple, interrelated uncertainties with significant feedback effects and time delays.

There are two generic types of management flight simulators. In some, you play against the computer, which has competitor strategies built into the workings of the game. In others, multiple players play the same game, each representing the key producers, customers, or regulators in the industry. In these games, the simulation determines how these different player strategies interact to drive industry evolution.

While management flight simulators can be used to help understand and potentially bound Level 3 uncertainties, they are often most valuable in Level 4 situations. When a market environment is so ambiguous that it is impossible to even bound the range of future outcomes, for instance, simulation games provide an efficient means to experiment with hundreds, if not thousands, of different assumptions for key uncertainties and company strategies. Any of these experiments may generate insight about the market without incurring the costs—and risks—of a real-world product or service experiment.

Playing these games over and over again also builds the pattern-recognition skills so crucial to crafting winning strategies under uncertainty. If you can use reference cases—both real and simulated—to spot emerging industry developments before competitors, you may be best positioned to capture significant first-mover advantages.

Finally, playing these games repeatedly helps managers train their minds to recognize and better understand the workings of dynamically complex business environments. The more managers play these games, the less likely they will be to miss important feedback effects and time delays when crafting their own strategies.

Strategists can choose to build management flight simulators from scratch, or they can rely on a set of canned games from system dynamics software vendors and consultants. McKinsey's system dynamics practice, for example, offers some twenty off-the-shelf simulation games covering a wide range of issues, from managing in cyclical industries and jump-starting profitable growth to shaping competitive dynamics and marketing and pricing new products.

Most companies should probably take a "real options" approach to investing in management flight simulators. Start with an existing game, and invest a small amount to partially tailor it to your market- and company-specific issues. If the game "takes" with your management team—helping it to see dynamically complex problems in a new light—"exercise" your option and develop new models specifically designed to help your company navigate through Level 4 uncertainty.

Recommended Readings

1. For a description of several different management flight simulators and applications to real organizations, see John Morecroft and John Sterman, eds., *Modeling for Learning Organizations* (Portland, OR: Productivity Press, 1994).

2. For a review of the literature on management flight simulators or microworlds, see Kim Warren and Paul Langley, "The Effective Communication of System Dynamics to Improve Insight and Learning in Management Education," *Journal of the Operational Research Society* 50, no. 4 (April 1999): 396–404.

3. To experiment with simple simulation models and identify various system dynamics training and consulting service options, see the Web sites for Ventana Systems (producer of Vensim modeling software), <http://www.vensim.com>, and High Performance Systems, Inc. (producer of ithink modeling software), <http://www.hps-inc.com>.

Notes

CHAPTER 1

1. Peter Coy, "Exploiting Uncertainty: The 'Real Options' Revolution in Decision-Making," *Business Week,* 7 June 1999, 118.
2. The typical process often includes sensitivity analyses to determine the impact of alternative assumptions on the strategy's expected return. In my experience, however, decision makers focus primarily on the base case forecasts when making their strategy choices.
3. Michael E. Porter, *Competitive Strategy: Techniques for Analyzing Industries and Competitors* (New York: The Free Press, 1980), 4.
4. I call this a binary view of uncertainty because it indicates that there are only two possible states of nature: certainty and uncertainty. With this binary view, uncertainty can be translated into a simple digital expression where 0 indicates uncertainty is "off" and 1 indicates uncertainty is "on."
5. Pankaj Ghemawat, *Strategy and the Business Landscape* (Reading, MA: Addison-Wesley, 1999), provides a concise overview of business strategy concepts and frameworks.
6. Most examples in this book are derived from real-world cases. Examples derived from McKinsey's consulting work, however, disguise company names and some aspects of the situation to maintain client confidentiality. In cases where a real company is named, the example was developed using only publicly available sources.

CHAPTER 2

1. Elements of the Alpha case have been borrowed from several different players in the industry to maintain client confidentiality.
2. Alpha was considering a network upgrade consisting of a move to a hybrid fiber coax architecture, which involved replacing much of the copper wire in the "last mile" of the network's connections with homes and businesses.

3. Throughout the book, I use the terms *four levels of residual uncertainty* and *four levels of uncertainty* interchangeably. Whenever I refer to one of the levels of uncertainty, please note that I am referring to residual uncertainty—the uncertainty that remains after the best possible analysis.

4. Titanium dioxide is a white pigment that is a key raw material in paints, plastics, and paper.

5. For more on the strategic interaction between Wal-Mart and Carrefour, see Richard Tomlinson, "Who's Afraid of Wal-Mart?" *Fortune,* 26 June 2000, 186–196.

6. For a brief, nontechnical overview of QUALCOMM's CDMA strategy, see Christine Y. Chen, "Qualcomm Hits the Big Time," *Fortune,* 15 May 2000, 213–229.

7. For more on the superjumbo-jet demand forecast and the superjumbo market in general, see Andy Reinhardt, "Boeing Gets Blown Sideways," *Business Week,* 16 October 2000, 62; "Chocks Away," *The Economist,* 29 July 2000, 58–59; "Thank You, Singapore," *The Economist,* 30 September 2000, 63–64; Jerry Useem, "Boeing Vs. Boeing," *Fortune,* 2 October 2000, 148–160; John Rossant, "Birth of a Giant," *Fortune,* 10 July 2000, 170–176.

8. See Bridget Eklund, "Broad Visions," *Red Herring,* July 2000, 296–299, for a summary of Enron's proposed bandwidth-trading strategy.

9. For a nontechnical introduction to the hybrid and fuel cell auto markets, see David Welch, "The Eco-Cars," *Business Week,* 14 August 2000, 62–68.

10. For a nontechnical overview of Celera's comparative genomics strategy, see David Stipp, "Celera, the Genome, and the Fruit-Fly Lady," *Fortune,* 10 July 2000, 148–151.

11. For an account of the formulation of Royal Dutch/Shell's renewable energy strategy, see Gary Hamel, *Leading the Revolution* (Boston: Harvard Business School Press, 2000), 175–184.

12. For more on strategic planning and decision making in such industries, see Shona L. Brown and Kathleen M. Eisenhardt, *Competing on the Edge: Strategy as Structured Chaos* (Boston: Harvard Business School Press, 1998).

CHAPTER 3

1. Chen, "Qualcomm Hits the Big Time," 218.

2. For more on the Calyx & Corolla strategy, see Walter J. Salmon and David Wylie, "Calyx & Corolla," Case 9-592-035 (Boston: Harvard Business School, 1995).

3. See Intermountain Health Care, "Medicine's Next Century," 1998 Annual Report, for more on Intermountain's integrated health care delivery strategy.

4. For more information on the Softsoap case, see Adam M. Brandenburger and Barry J. Nalebuff, *Co-opetition* (New York: Currency Doubleday, 1996), 149–151.

5. *Business Week* had this to say about the Motorola–General Instrument merger: "The deal even comes with a sweetener. General Instrument also brings know-how for DSL (digital subscriber lines), a technology to provide broadband service over copper telephone wire. GI holds a majority stake in Next Level Communications Inc., a high-profile maker of DSL gear. So Motorola is now positioned on both sides of the broadband race. 'That's the hidden jewel,' [Motorola CEO Christopher B.] Galvin says." See Roger O. Crockett, "Has Motorola Found Its Cable Guy?" *Business Week,* 27 September 1999, 50, for more on the Motorola–General Instrument merger.

6. Capital One Financial Corporation, "The Innovation Imperative," 1998 Annual Report, 4.

7. Capital One is rewriting the rules of the credit game in these markets. "In the United Kingdom and Canada, we're winning customers with innovative products that are slashing the price of credit cards—a major consumer benefit in markets long dominated by banks charging 20% or more," argued Capital One in "The Innovation Imperative," 10.

8. Gary Hamel and C. K. Prahalad, *Competing for the Future* (Boston: Harvard Business School Press, 1994), 19–20.

9. James C. Collins and Jerry I. Porras, *Built to Last: Successful Habits of Visionary Companies* (New York: HarperBusiness, 1994), 140.

10. Brown and Eisenhardt, *Competing on the Edge,* 147.

11. Jin-Goon Kim, Olivier Sibony, and Jayant Sinha, "Shaping New Markets," unpublished research, McKinsey & Company, Boston, MA, 1999.

12. The research applied the following filters to the 1,126 U.S. single-business companies (report only one business segment in filings submitted to the U.S. Securities and Exchange Commission) in the Compustat database in 1995: They had at least $25 million in sales in 1985, they grew at least 5 percent faster than their industry peers for at least six of the ten years between 1985 and 1995, and they increased their market capitalization by at least 10 percent per year between 1985 and 1995. These filters identified sixty-two companies from which the top fifty companies in annual sales growth were chosen for further analysis. These were truly high-growth stars, averaging 37 percent sales growth per annum between 1985 and 1995. And while they represented only 4 percent of the Compustat sample, they accounted for 23 percent of the sales growth, 29 percent of the net operating profit growth, and 40 percent of the job creation.

13. This example is developed in greater detail in Coy, "Exploiting Uncertainty," 118–124.

14. See, for example, Porter, *Competitive Strategy.*

15. For more information on Kodak's digital photography strategy and its likelihood of success, see William Symonds, "Fisher's Photo Finish," *Business Week,* 21 June 1999, 34; Geoffrey Smith, "Film vs. Digital: Can Kodak Build a Bridge," *Business Week,* 2 August 1999, 66–68; Geoffrey Smith, "Will Kodak's Carp Miss His Photo Op?" *Business Week,* 9 October 2000, 52.

16. The key to making the right choice in abandoning an old business system for a new one lies in understanding what is the correct base case. The correct base case is rarely business value as usual in periods of rapid, discontinuous change. Suppose a business is valued at 100 today. It is a lot easier to accept a new business system model that promises to deliver 90 tomorrow if the next best alternative is sticking to the existing business model and earning 80. Business decision makers in this case will make the right choice if they understand that the relevant base case valuation is 80, not 100.

17. This list of successful shaper attributes and examples comes from John Hagel, Joe Heel, Somu Subramaniam, and Lo-Ping Yeh, unpublished research (New York: McKinsey & Company, 1996–1997).

18. Recall the McKinsey research that showed that 86 percent of the biggest business "stars" between 1985 and 1995 followed predominantly shaping strategies.

19. Obviously, this exercise is a bit unfair since we are examining these strategy choices with the advantage of 20/20 hindsight. The companies, on the other hand, could only rely on 20/20 foresight, at best, when making their choices. Nonetheless, this exercise provides a useful illustration of how to use the checklist to test your assumptions and thus avoid making mistakes that are common when relying on more free-form approaches to decision making.

20. Stephanie Stoughton, "Circuit City's Slipped Disk," *The Washington Post,* 17 June 1999, provides a nice overview of the failed Divx strategy.

21. See Brandenburger and Nalebuff, *Co-opetition,* (149–151, 242–244), for more information on the Minnetonka Softsoap case.

22. John Schwartz, "Iridium Files for Chapter 11," *The Washington Post,* 14 August 1999.

23. See Roger O. Crockett, "Why Motorola Should Hang Up on Iridium," *Business Week,* 30 August 1999, 46, for more on the economics of Iridium's network.

24. Schwartz, "Iridium Files for Chapter 11."

25. Or did they? Iridium may still rise from the ashes. On November 22, 2000, Iridium Satellite LLC, of Arnold, Maryland, purchased its satellite assets. Just weeks later, Iridium secured a $72 million satellite telephone contract with the U.S. government that has options worth up to $252 million.

CHAPTER 4

1. Stoughton, "Circuit City's Slipped Disk."

2. Clayton M. Christensen, *The Innovator's Dilemma: When New Technologies Cause Great Firms to Fail* (Boston: Harvard Business School Press, 1997).

3. Rita Gunther McGrath and Ian MacMillan suggest that this might have been a more effective approach for Iridium. Rita Gunther McGrath and Ian MacMillan, *The Entrepreneurial Mindset: Strategies for Continuously Creating Opportunity in an Age of Uncertainty* (Boston: Harvard Business School Press, 2000), 169–170.

4. While there are many good sources available on how to define and recognize real options, this section was influenced most by McKinsey research led by Tom

Copeland and Max Michaels. Publications that summarize this work include: Keith J. Leslie and Max P. Michaels, "The Real Power of Real Options," *The McKinsey Quarterly,* no. 3 (1997): 4–22; Thomas E. Copeland and Philip T. Keenan, "How Much Is Flexibility Worth?" *The McKinsey Quarterly,* no. 2 (1998): 38–49; Thomas E. Copeland and Philip T. Keenan, "Making Real Options Real," *The McKinsey Quarterly,* no. 3 (1998): 128–141.

5. The fact that growth, insurance, and learning options are not mutually exclusive should not hinder your company's ability to recognize real options. It is not necessarily important to cleanly categorize any given action as a growth, insurance, or learning option. What is important, however, is that your company actively considers a full range of actions that build in the flexibility to reinvest, divest, and/or invest as the market environment evolves. An attempt to categorize each potential action as a growth, insurance, or learning option helps a company diagnose whether or not it has built flexibility in on all three possible dimensions—reinvestment, divestment, and investment.

6. The concept of leverage is easy to apply to growth and learning options. For insurance options, however, it is a bit more complex. The following two rules should help. First, insurance options that provide flexibility to easily switch strategic direction should be low cost relative to the cost of building a diversified business or strategy portfolio that provides the same degree of flexibility. Second, insurance options that provide flexibility to scale down strategies should be low cost relative to expected divestment costs without the option.

7. The newspaper Web site and radio spectrum auction examples come from Petri Allas, David McDonald, Max Michaels, and Ramesh Venkataraman, unpublished research, McKinsey, London, 1996.

8. Of course, if the property is easy to resell, without incurring substantial transaction costs, this is a relatively small bet, with limited sunk costs.

9. In one very special case, the answer is easy. A real option will always be preferred to a big bet if it maintains the same upside payoffs. By limiting irreversible commitments, the real option has better downside payoffs than the big bet. If it has better downside payoffs, and equal upside payoffs, the real option is obviously a better alternative.

10. There are actually six drivers of option value. Each will be identified in greater detail in the next section on quantitative ROV methods. However, four of these six drivers only affect the value of options, and not big bets, and thus they cleanly differentiate between big bet and real option alternatives. These are the four drivers highlighted in this section.

11. After this example was developed, and as the book went into production, Boeing announced that it was scrapping plans for the 747X altogether. Thus Boeing has further scaled back its interest in the superjumbo market at this time. For more background on the superjumbo case, see "Thank You, Singapore," 63–64; "Chocks Away," 58–59; and Reinhardt, "Boeing Gets Blown Sideways," 62.

12. "Thank You, Singapore," 63.

13. Reinhardt, "Boeing Gets Blown Sideways," 62.

14. Ibid.
15. "Thank You, Singapore," 63. The A3XX in this quote refers to the Airbus A380 superjumbo-jet.
16. Information on KCube comes from the author's interviews with Max Michaels, president and CEO of KCube, fall 2000.
17. For a nontechnical summary of this case, see Pankaj Ghemawat, *Games Businesses Play: Cases and Models* (Cambridge: MIT Press, 1997), 59–86.
18. Ghemawat, *Games Businesses Play,* 68.
19. Ibid.
20. This example is adapted from Leslie and Michaels, "The Real Power of Real Options," 4–22.
21. As subsequently modified by Robert Merton to account for dividend payments, in "Theory of Rational Option Pricing," *Bell Journal of Economics and Management Science* 4, no. 2 (1973): 141–183.
22. $V = Se^{-\delta t} * \{N(d_1)\} - Xe^{-rt} * \{N(d_2)\}$, where $d_1 = \{\ln(S/X) + (r - \delta + \sigma^2/2) * t\}/\{\sigma * \sqrt{t}\}$, $d_2 = d_1 - \sigma * \sqrt{t}$, V = option value, S = stock price, X = exercise price, δ = dividend rate, r = risk-free interest rate, σ = uncertainty, t = option duration, and N(d) = cumulative normal probability distribution function. See any M.B.A.-level finance textbook for more details on the Black-Scholes option-pricing formula.
23. Coy, "Exploiting Uncertainty: The 'Real Options' Revolution in Decision-Making," 122.
24. The Biogen Avonex case is developed in Aswath Damodaran, "The Promise of Real Options," *Journal of Applied Corporate Finance* 13, no. 2 (Summer 2000): 29–44.
25. The mathematics to prove this result, however, is fairly cumbersome. For this reason, I discuss only the intuition for the result in the text. Those interested in how to explicitly calculate the value of deferral options should consult specialized real option texts, including Lenos Trigeorgis, *Real Options: Managerial Flexibility and Strategy in Resource Allocation* (Cambridge: MIT Press, 1996); Martha Amram and Nalin Kulatilaka, *Real Options: Managing Strategic Investment in an Uncertain World* (Boston: Harvard Business School Press, 1999).
26. That said, financial option-pricing models like Black-Scholes provide technically correct valuations of real options only in very special circumstances under a very strict set of assumptions. In my experience, however, using these models to approximate real option value often leads to "directionally correct" estimates that point strategists toward the right real option versus big bet choices. There are alternatives, of course, to these approximate approaches. First, real option valuation models can be built from the ground up to specify all the valuation nuances in a particular setting. Second, and at the other extreme, strategists can rely on the qualitative rules for sorting out real option and big bet choices that were introduced in the previous section if they are concerned about "garbage in, garbage out" modeling efforts. Those that wish to build specific models from the ground up would be wise to consult a real options expert and some of the following sources before getting started: Trigeorgis, *Real Options: Managerial*

Flexibility and Strategy in Resource Allocation; Amram and Kulatilaka, *Real Options: Managing Strategic Investment in an Uncertain World;* Tom Copeland, Tim Koller, and Jack Murrin, *Valuation: Measuring and Managing the Value of Companies,* 3rd ed. (New York: John Wiley & Sons, 2000), 395–425; Martha Amram and Nalin Kulatilaka, "Strategy and Shareholder Value Creation: The Real Options Frontier," *Journal of Applied Corporate Finance* 13, no. 2 (Summer 2000): 15–28; Damodaran, "The Promise of Real Options," 29–44.

27. I have ignored a number of difficult technical issues—including the appropriate discount rate to use in the decision tree—in order to clarify key conceptual issues in the Acme case. Per note 26, I encourage you to consult real options experts and texts in order to better understand these issues before beginning your own ROV applications.

CHAPTER 5

1. This may not be true for investors like Warren Buffet, who may move markets with the sheer size and credibility of their investment decisions.

2. Brown and Eisenhardt, *Competing on the Edge,* 6; Brandenburger and Nalebuff, *Co-opetition,* 15–16.

3. John Hagel III and Marc Singer, *Net Worth: Shaping Markets When Customers Make the Rules* (Boston: Harvard Business School Press, 1999), 141–142.

4. David H. Maister and D. Daryl Wyckoff, "Federal Express Corporation (A)," Case 9-674-093 (Boston: Harvard Business School, 1974).

5. See the case discussion in chapter 3 for more details on why the Divx strategy failed.

6. Circuit City did have to make some concessions, however, to consumers. First, it dropped prices on Divx players and disks to sell off its inventory. Second, it allowed customers who had purchased Divx players in the sixty days prior to its announcement to close the business one of the following options: a $100 rebate, an outright exchange or refund, or a refund of the difference between the price paid and current prices. See Stoughton, "Circuit City's Slipped Disk," for more details.

7. See, for example, Brandon Copple, "Stepping in It," *Forbes,* 21 August 2000, 56–57; Paul Raeburn, "Warning: Biotech Is Hurting Itself," *Business Week,* 20 December 1999, 78.

8. Hamel, *Leading the Revolution,* 175–184.

9. Ibid., 140.

10. Collins and Porras, *Built to Last,* 140.

11. Ari de Geus, *The Living Company: Habits for Survival in a Turbulent Business Environment* (Boston: Harvard Business School Press, 1997), 143.

12. Michael Moeller, "Who Do You Want to Buy Today?" *Business Week,* 7 June 1999, 33.

13. Jim Collins, "Built to Flip," *Fast Company,* no. 32 (March 2000), 131.

14. Max Michaels, conversation with author, 12 October 2000.
15. Ibid.
16. Eric D. Beinhocker, "Robust Adaptive Strategies," *Sloan Management Review* 40, no. 3 (1999): 96.

CHAPTER 6

1. The five tools covered in the appendix are scenario planning, game theory, decision analysis, system dynamics models, and management flight simulators. In addition, chapter 4 covers ROV models.
2. A reminder: MECE stands for "mutually exclusive, collectively exhaustive." Under Level 2 uncertainty, by definition, one can identify a set of possible future outcomes, and one and only one of the scenarios in that set will occur. For more on MECE and the definition of Level 2 uncertainty, see chapter 2.
3. Any basic textbook on decision analysis will contain numerous examples of event and decision trees. I recommend Robert T. Clemen, *Making Hard Decisions: An Introduction to Decision Analysis,* 2nd ed. (Pacific Grove, CA: Duxbury Press, 1996); David C. Skinner, *Introduction to Decision Analysis: A Practitioner's Guide to Improving Decision Quality,* 2nd ed. (Gainesville, FL: Probabilistic Publishing, 1999).
4. Assume there are two scenarios, A and B, and the probability of A occurring is P_a while the probability of B occurring is P_b. Suppose a strategy generates payoffs of X_a in scenario A, and X_b in scenario B. Then the expected value of this strategy is $P_a*X_a + P_b*X_b$. In words, the expected value is the probability-weighted average of payoffs. For more on expected value and other basic statistical concepts used in decision analysis—including variance, standard deviation, medians, and modes—consult any introductory statistics textbook.
5. Companies in more stable environments should master the Level 1 and Level 2 toolkits before investing much time on Levels 3 and 4. High-technology companies, on the other hand, may want to focus their initial efforts on Levels 3 and 4.

CHAPTER 7

1. Yogi Berra, "Yogi Berra: The Official Web Site from LTD Enterprises, a Berra Family Corporation," <http://www.yogi-berra.com> (accessed 18 December 2000).
2. See Henry Mintzberg, *The Rise and Fall of Strategic Planning* (New York: The Free Press, 1994), for a far-reaching critique of traditional strategic-planning approaches, particularly their inability to adequately address turbulent business environments. In an article summarizing this work, Mintzberg wrote, "According to the premises of strategic planning, the world is supposed to hold still while a plan is being developed and then stay on the predicted course while that plan is being implemented." "The Fall and Rise of Strategic Planning," *Harvard Business Review* 72, no. 1 (January–February 1994): 110.

3. Berra, "Yogi Berra: The Official Web Site from LTD Enterprises, a Berra Family Corporation."

4. The Financo case is based primarily on one financial services company's experiences, but elements from similar experiences in different industries have been blended into the case to retain anonymity.

5. Ram Charan, "Managing Through Chaos," *Fortune,* 23 November 1998, 283–290, quotes on 284. This article discusses Reed's trip wire system and other methods for managing in uncertain times.

6. Timothy A. Luehrman, "Investment Opportunities as Real Options," *Harvard Business Review* 76, no. 4 (July–August 1998): 51–67; Timothy A. Luehrman, "Strategy as a Portfolio of Real Options," *Harvard Business Review* 76, no. 5 (September–October 1998): 89–99.

7. Nancy A. Nichols, "Scientific Management at Merck: An Interview with CFO Judy Lewent," *Harvard Business Review* 72, no. 1 (January–February 1994): 89–99.

8. These two paragraphs on Enron's use of real options thinking are based on Coy, "Exploiting Uncertainty: The 'Real Options' Revolution in Decision-Making," 120.

9. Max Michaels, conversation with author, 12 October 2000.

10. The concepts and many of the case examples covered in this section were developed during an unpublished McKinsey research effort led by Shona Brown, Michael Dickstein, Chandru Krishnamurthy, Alex Rogers, and Patrick Viguerie. This effort developed case studies on companies like Microsoft, Intel, Cisco, Charles Schwab, Compaq, and BellSouth, focusing on how they developed and managed strategies in highly uncertain, Level 4 environments.

11. Andy Serwer, "There's Something About Cisco," *Fortune,* 15 May 2000, 128.

12. Quentin Hardy, "Lighting Up Nortel," *Forbes,* 21 August 2000, 53.

13. Brown and Eisenhardt, *Competing on the Edge,* 147.

14. Thomas A. Stewart, "Making Decisions in Real Time," *Fortune,* 26 June 2000, 332–334; Serwer, "There's Something About Cisco," 128.

15. "We identified several common traits among businesses that experiment effectively. One is that their managers have a simple and clearly defined vision of the business in the future. They do not try to predict any particular future of the industry, but rather they try to define their business' identity within whatever future comes." Brown and Eisenhardt, *Competing on the Edge,* 148.

16. Quotes for this example come from Capital One Financial Corporation, "The Innovation Imperative," 4.

17. Capital One Financial Corporation, "The Innovation Imperative."

18. Brown and Eisenhardt's "time pacing" concept is helpful in setting the right "rhythm" for time-based planning and decision making. See Brown and Eisenhardt, *Competing on the Edge,* 161–188.

19. See Richard Foster and Sarah Kaplan, *Creative Destruction: Why Companies That Are Built to Last Underperform the Market—And How to Successfully Transform Them* (New York: Currency Doubleday, 2001), 261–287 for more on FrameworkS.

20. See Hamel, *Leading the Revolution,* 243–275.

APPENDIX

1. When the process and end product objectives are not aligned, managers can find scenario-planning exercises extremely frustrating. Managers with a real-time strategy decision to make find mind-set–shifting scenario development an academic exercise that distracts them from the decision at hand. On the other hand, managers looking to expand their management team's collective mind-set find decision-driven scenario development too narrow and unlikely to spur creative thought. Most managers would find scenario-planning exercises much more helpful if they aligned the scenario techniques with their objectives.

2. Scenario planners use a variety of different techniques to identify these correlations. The sources in the recommended readings section provide details on these techniques.

3. This case and figure A-1 are from Peter Schwartz and James A. Oglivy, "Plotting Your Scenarios," in *Learning from the Future: Competitive Foresight Scenarios,* eds. Liam Fahey and Robert M. Randall (New York: John Wiley & Sons, 1998), 57–80.

4. This section is based on Hugh Courtney, "Games Managers Should Play," *World Economic Affairs* 2, no. 1 (Autumn 1997): 48–49.

5. As long as each player has a consistent set of objectives and is aligning actions with those objectives, these game theory methods will provide valuable insight on likely player actions. If, however, a player acts randomly with no consistent set of objectives and actions, then game theory is probably not the right tool (although, in this case, there really would be no substitute tool, besides perhaps a crystal ball).

6. This is a simplified and disguised version of a real-world case. I use it as an example here because its general structure and results are similar to many market entry "games."

7. Game theorists call that situation where each player is content with its strategy given the strategies other players are following a Nash equilibrium.

8. See the decision analysis textbooks in the recommended readings section for a more thorough overview of the broad range of decision analysis tools.

9. Flexor is a hybrid case that includes elements from several different industrial companies. Johan Ahlberg, Henrik Arwidi, Bill Barnett, and I originally developed this case for an internal McKinsey training course.

10. This is assuming that Flexor cares only about the financial payoffs summarized in table A-1. If Flexor's decision-making criteria were multidimensional—with simultaneous interests in financial payoffs, employment, or other characteristics of the strategies—Flexor would have to assign relative weightings to each characteristic to reach its decision (unless, of course, it had the unlikely occurrence that the rankings of each strategy were consistent across each decision-making criterion). Senior management team workshops can be extremely useful in achieving consensus on the weights assigned to alternative criteria.

11. See chapter 6, note 5, for an explanation of expected value.

12. Let X be the probability of scenario B. Then licensing technology B has a higher expected value than selling the business if $40*(1 - X) + 100*X > 80$. Using simple algebra to solve for X, this implies $X > .67$, or 67 percent.

13. How does one determine certainty equivalents? Theoretically, they can be derived from the underlying "utility functions" that determine decision makers' tolerance for risk. In practical terms, one can surface certainty equivalents during decision-maker workshops that ask attendees to estimate how much of the company's money they would be willing to bet to play lotteries that have the same payoff profiles (payoffs and probabilities) as the strategies they are considering. These certainty equivalents can then be discussed and debated by the decision-making team until consensus is reached, or until the ultimate decision maker, if there is one, makes up his mind.

14. A *probability density function* (pdf) describes the probability of every point within a range of possible outcomes. For most of this book, I have assumed that it is possible to identify the pdf under Level 2 uncertainty, but impossible to do so under Level 3. This assumption allowed me to better clarify the expected differences between Levels 2 and 3 uncertainty for most practitioners. However, it is true that one interpretation of Level 3 uncertainty—the range of possible outcomes can be identified, but not a limited set of scenarios within this range—does not preclude situations where the pdf can be identified. Therefore, in rare cases, even strategists facing Level 3 uncertainty will be able to define the probability of every possible future outcome. To use the Black-Scholes option-pricing formula to value real options in chapter 4, for example, we had to implicitly assume that the Level 3 uncertainty over an option's cash flows could be described by a well-defined pdf (the lognormal distribution). These and similar technical details are beyond the scope of this book, and they are also of limited value to most business practitioners. Interested readers can learn more by studying academic real option sources (some are referenced in the notes for chapter 4) and advanced statistics textbooks. In addition, the textbooks in the recommended readings section identify decision analysis approaches that can be used under Level 3 uncertainty when the pdf is known.

15. This case is reported in Andrew Doman, Maurice A. Glucksman, Nhuoc-Lan Tu, and Kim Warren, "The Talent-Growth Dynamic," *The McKinsey Quarterly*, no. 1 (2000): 106–115.

16. See the Web sites for Ventana Systems (producer of Vensim modeling software), <http://www.vensim.com>, and High Performance Systems, Inc. (producer of ithink modeling software), <http://www.hps-inc.com>.

17. See Paul A. Langley, Hendrik Sabert, and Paolo Timoni, "Going Mobile," *The McKinsey Quarterly*, no. 1 (2000): 52–61.

Index

About the Author

Hugh Courtney is an Associate Principal with McKinsey & Company, where he coleads its Global Strategy Practice. Dr. Courtney serves clients across a wide range of industry sectors, focusing on strategic decision making under high uncertainty and in concentrated markets. He has published several applied pieces on these topics, including articles in the *Harvard Business Review* and *The McKinsey Quarterly*. Dr. Courtney earned his Ph.D. from the Massachusetts Institute of Technology, and he was an economics professor before joining McKinsey.